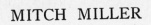
MITCH MILLER

STARVED ROCK

TOWARDS THE GULF

THE GREAT VALLEY

SONGS AND SATIRES

SPOON RIVER ANTHOLOGY
WITH ADDITIONAL POEMS

MITCH MILLER

BY

EDGAR LEE MASTERS

AUTHOR OF
STARVED ROCK, SPOON RIVER
ANTHOLOGY, ETC., ETC.

WITH ILLUSTRATIONS BY
JOHN SLOAN

New York

THE MACMILLAN COMPANY

1920

All rights reserved

Norwood Press
J. S. Cushing Co. — Berwick & Smith Co.
Norwood, Mass., U.S.A.

TO

MY LITTLE DAUGHTERS

MADELINE AND MARCIA

MITCH MILLER

SUPPOSIN' you was lyin' in a room and was asleep or pretty near asleep; and bein' asleep you could hear people talkin' but it didn't mean nothin' to you — just talk; and you kind of knew things was goin' on around you, but still you was way off in your sleep and belonged to yourself as a sleeper, and what was goin' on didn't make no difference to you; and really, supposin' you was tryin' to get back into deeper sleep before you heard these things. And then, supposin' now and then as your eyes rolled back into your head while sleepin' you saw through the lids — not tryin' to look, but your eyes just saw as they rolled past the open place between the lids — and you saw squares of light and dark, or maybe roundish blurs. And then supposin' sometimes you heard a noise, and as it turned out it was somebody goin' in and out of the room, or somebody closin' or openin' a door. And supposin' these here people were not tip-toein' exactly, but were kind of watchin' and laughin' a little maybe to see what you would do when you woke up. And finally one of your eyes kind of opened and you saw your ma sittin' in the corner, sewin', or peelin' apples maybe; and you saw your pa goin' out

MITCH MILLER

B   I

of a door, and your sister came up to you and looked clost to see when you was goin' to wake up. And supposin' after a bit you sat up and rubbed your eyes, and looked around and you was in a room, and the room was in your ma's house, and your ma sat there, sure enough, and your pa was goin' out of the door, and your sister was lookin' at you. And supposin' then you went out-doors and there was a yard and you saw the house from the outside, and there was a house near and other houses, and a fence in front, and wagons goin' by and people. And then supposin' by and by you found out that a railroad ran right by the side fence, and a great big black thing makin' a noise and blowin' out smoke came close to the fence sometimes, and a man would be ridin' in a little house on top of this big black thing, who talked to you, and laughed when you showed him a pipe made out of a cork and a match, and a cherry-seed put in a hollowed-out place of the cork for tobacco.

And then supposin' other children came around, and finally you went out on to a side-walk and saw lots of houses, and by and by ran away and saw stores all around a lovely square and a great court house in the center. And supposin' you found out that there was a river just under the hills you could see beyond the railroad, and by and by you heard your folks say Petersburg; and by and by you knew that was the name of this town. And sometimes you could see more of the town, because your grandpa and grandma came with a carriage and drove clear through the town so as to get to the country and out to the farm where they lived.

And then supposin' one day all the things in the house was loaded on a wagon and you rode with your ma up the hill to a better house and a bigger yard with oak trees, and the things were put in the house and you began to live here, and saw different houses around, and different children came to play; and supposin' there was a girl named Cooster McCoy that used to come to the fence and make faces and say awful words which your ma told you was wicked and would make God punish you if you said 'em: and then supposin' you began to hear your pa and ma talk of Mr. Miller and what a wonderful man he was, and Mrs. Miller and what a good woman she was, and about the Miller girls, how funny and smart they was, and about Mitch Miller, the wonderfulest boy in town. And supposin' you went with your ma to visit 'em and when you got there you saw Mr. Miller readin' to Mrs. Miller, and you saw the Miller girls playin', and you saw Mitch Miller chewin' gum and readin' a book, and was so taken with the book he wouldn't play with you, but finally said he'd read to you, and so began to read from a book which he said was "Tom Sawyer," which was all about a boy just our age. And supposin' you got the book after a while and you read it too, but you understood it only because after a while Mitch explained it to you.

Well, this is the way it began: first the room, then the house — then the town in a way — and then Mitch — but I got acquainted with him really and he became my friend as I tell about after a while. Only now I just tell how things began to clear up as I came out of sleep, as you might say.

And onct when I was up to Mr. Miller's and he was readin' from Shakespeare to Mrs. Miller he came to a place where it says, "Our little life is rounded by a sleep." I remember this because Mr. Miller stopped and began to talk about it; and Mitch looked up from

readin' " Tom Sawyer," and I began to think about the
sleep I came out of, and how things at first seemed
kind of double and like you had taken so-and-so's cure
for consumption which ma says has opium in it. For
when I took it for a cold, things kind of swum around
me like a circular looking-glass, that you could see
through somehow, and everything seemed kind of way
off and funny and somethin' to laugh at and not treat
as real.

Well, at first, too, everything seemed alive — even
sticks and stones; and the broomstick I made into a
gun seemed to have a life or kind of a memory of somethin'. And when I told Mr. Miller this he says, you're
a savage, or you've been one in some other life, or else
maybe you're repeatin' the life of a savage, and he
called it filogenesis, or somethin' like that.

But anyway, your town comes to you at last; at
least the town as it is then and seems to you then with
all the folks in it, and your relatives, and all their ways
and all the stories about 'em. And you get your place
and find your friends, and you find one friend as I found
Mitch. And so you're awake, or as much awake, we'll
say, as you are at first in the morning when you first
stretch out of bed. And so you get ready for the day
and the next sleep ——

CHAPTER I

I GOT acquainted with Mitch this way : In the first place when we moved to Petersburg and got into our house and was settled, one day Bob Pendleton came to see me. He said he'd come to call—that's the word he used. You see right in front of our house was Mr. Montgomery's house — an awful big brick house, with a big yard ; and the back of it was in front of our house with a tall hedge ; but there was a place to go through the hedge, through a grape arbor up to the house, and around to the front yard. Next to Mr. Montgomery's yard was Bucky Gum's pasture where he kept his cows. But if you stood down by the pasture away from Mr. Montgomery's hedge, you could look across and see Mr. Pendleton's fine brick house where Bob, this boy, lived. Mr. Pendleton kept a store and a bank and was awful rich ; and when Bob came to call on me my ma was tickled most to death. She wanted me to have nice friends, boys who would grow up and be prominent in the world. And when Bob first came she went to the door and let him in and then came to me and made me wash and comb my hair. So I went in and here was Bob.

He had on a new suit and shiny shoes and a bow neck-tie, and he had a little ring on his finger. But he was so thin that he had to stand up twice to make a shadow. So he set there and nothin' much was said. I was afraid to ask him to swing, or to go to the barn, or anything.

5

By and by he asked me if I had read "Little Men."
I said no. Then he asked me if I had read the Pansy
series. I said no to that; then he asked me if I sub-
scribed to "Our Youth," which was a boys' paper full
of good stories about nice girls and boys. I'd never heard
of it. Then he asked me if I liked to play ball, and of
course I did. And he said he had a ball ground in his
orchard and to come over some time. Myrtle, my sister,
liked nice boys, but she thought Bob was not the right
kind of nice. But ma urged the friendship on me. And
so it began.

And I must say Bob was a good boy, and I have no
complaints to make; but I didn't know Mitch then,
and so didn't see the difference so much. Well, Bob
liked me and he kept havin' me over to his house. He
had a big yard with trees in it, and a fountain with a
stone figure of a little boy, not much clothes on, holdin'
an urn. Bob's pa was the leadin' member of the Baptist Church and awful strict; and as Mitch's father
was a Congregational preacher, Mr. Pendleton didn't
like him on account of differin' with him about baptism.

Bob's house was just full of fine things — oil paint-
ings of his father and mother, his sisters and himself;
fine furniture all in horsehair; lots of silver for the table;
and they kept two girls and had had 'em for years;
and Mrs. Pendleton watched Bob very careful so he
wouldn't catch cold or anything, because he had a
weak chest. And Bob would take me down to his
father's store where we got raisins and candy, and we
played ball in the orchard.

Everything Bob had was brand new, and you had to
be careful of it. He had a new ball; and on the day I
met Mitch we was pitchin' ball — Bob and me, in the

orchard — and Bob kept saying to be careful and not let it roll in the grass or get in the mud, that he wanted to keep it white and clean. Well, of course, I missed now and then and Bob seemed displeased. And when it rolled into the mud he came up and took the ball and wiped it off and looked mad. Just then he said: "There comes that Mitch Miller, and I think we'd better quit playin' anyway." I knew Mitch's name and had seen him, but we hadn't run together yet.

Mitch climbed over the fence into the orchard, and Bob began to kind a move away. I could see that Bob didn't want him, for he said, "Come on, Arthur." Everybody called me Skeet, though my name was Arthur, which I hated. Bob always called me Arthur and made me call him Robert, though his nick-

MITCH CLIMBED OVER THE FENCE

name was "Shadder." When Bob said to come on to me, Mitch says, "Wait a minute, Skeet, I've somethin' to tell you." So I said to Bob, "Wait a minute, Robert," and Bob said, "You're comin' now or not at all." That made me mad, so I stood there. Bob went on and Mitch came up.

"Let him go," said Mitch. "You don't care, do you?"

"Not much," says I.

"Well, I hope not," says Mitch. "He's a sissy — spoiled by his ma. And you don't call this any fun, do you, pitchin' ball with a ball so good that you dassn't let it roll on the ground? Now, I've seen you around, Skeet, and I like you, and if you like me, we'll be chums, and go havers on everything, and if anybody fights you he'll have to fight me, and the same way with me, and I'll bet we'll have more fun together in a day than you could have with Shadder Pendleton in a year. Do you agree?" I said, "Yes, I agree," for I liked Mitch — I liked his name, I liked his way, and his face, his voice, everything about him right then; and I knew what I was promisin'.

Mitch says, "Do you want to have some fun?" I says, "You bet I do."

"Well," Mitch says, "there's more goin' on in this town than you ever saw, if you only keep your eyes open. But I'll bet Shadder never hears of it, and if you run with him you'll never hear of it either. Do you know what's goin' to happen to-day?" "No," says I.

"Well," says Mitch, "Jack Plunkett, who was town marshal here once, and Ruddy Hedgpeth are goin' to have a fight to see which can whip the other."

"Where?" says I.

"Down near Old Salem," says Mitch, "on the flat sand by the river, clost to the mill. And I want to see it, and so do you."

"You bet I want to see it," I said.

So Mitch went on to tell me that Jack Plunkett had never been whipped and neither had Ruddy Hedgpeth. They had whipped everybody but each other. And each said he could whip the other. And last Saturday

Ruddy was in town and went around the square sayin'
he could whip Jack, and Jack heard it and sent back
word he'd fight him a week off, on a Saturday, and this
is the Saturday. And Mitch said we'd better hurry so
as to get there before the fight was over, Old Salem
bein' about a mile from town.

By this time Shadder had walked out of the orchard
and was pretty near to the house and Mitch said, "Now
he's gone, let him go, and come on. If he ever says you
left him, you can say he left you, for he did."

It was a spring day — it was April — and we walked
as fast as we could, runnin' part of the time. Mitch
was wild about the country, about trees, birds, the
river and the fields. And he whistled and sang. On
the way out he began to talk to me about "Tom Sawyer,"
and asked me if I had read the book. This was one of
the books I *had* read; so I said so. And Mitch says,
"Do you know we can do exactly what Tom Sawyer
and Huck Finn did?"

"What's that?" I said.

"Why, find treasure. It's just as surely here as
anything. Of course there ain't no caves around here,
at least I don't know of any. But think of the old houses
— look at that old house down there by the ravine that
goes into the river across from Mr. Morris' wagon shop.
Think of those old houses clost to the Baptist Church;
and think of the dead limbs on the trees in Montgomery's woods. But of course if we go into this, no one
must know what we are doin'. We must keep still and
if they catch us diggin', we must lie. If you don't know
how to lie very well, Skeet, just listen to me and foller
the story I tell."

I agreed to this. And Mitch went on.

"And by and by, we'll find treasure and divide it, for I have taken you for my chum and half of mine is yours, and a half of yours is mine."

By this time we had come to a pretty high bank about a hundred yards from the mill. We heard voices and looked down on the sand bank, and there were about fifty men sittin' or standin' around. And there was my

LOOKING DOWN ON THE SAND BANK

pa. So I says, "I can't go down there, Mitch, my pa will whip me or drive me away. I know for certain he wouldn't want me to see this." "Well," says Mitch, "what's the difference? We're not more'n 75 feet away from 'em and can see everything and hear everything if there's anything to hear. So let's just lie down here in the grass and take it easy, and look down on 'em and watch it." So we did. There seemed to be some arrangin' of things. My pa seemed to be standin' clost to Ruddy Hedgpeth and talkin' to him and kind of advisin' him or takin' care of him. And George Montgomery was doin' the same for Jack Plunkett. Mitch says, "They're the seconds."

"What's that?" says I.

"Why," says Mitch, "seconds see that everything is fair, and no foolin'."

We could hear most everything they said, and they were talkin' about whether Jack Plunkett could choke Ruddy Hedgpeth if he got him. My pa said not; and Jack Plunkett said it was a fight to see who could whip the other, and if he got Ruddy so he could lay his hands on him and choke him until he gave up, that was fair and he insisted on it. Then Ruddy and my pa stepped to one side and talked secret; and then my pa said out loud that it was all right, and chokin' would not be barred; but of course what one could do, the other could. Jack Plunkett laughed at this an awful mockin' laugh, because he was the most terrible choker in the county and felt he could get the best of anybody in a chokin' match.

Then Jack and Ruddy began to undress, that is, they took off everything but their pants. Jack had a beard and a big square face, and a chest as thick as a horse and arms as big as a man's legs. And Ruddy was about as big only a little shorter, but he wore no beard, but his face and chest looked clean and slick and he was known to be an awful hard hitter. Then they got out on a flat place, level and hard sand, and began, my pa and George Montgomery takin' care of them and about fifty others watchin' as I said.

They stood and eyed each other and walked around and watched for a chance. Pretty soon Ruddy hit Jack on the chin and sent his head back and Jack rushed on Ruddy and got his hands on him, but Ruddy slipped away. Then Jack hit Ruddy, and Ruddy kind of wheeled around; and Jack rushed for Ruddy again, and again got his hands on him, but they slipped off. Then they seemed to get close together and just pound each other; and pretty soon Ruddy hit Jack and knocked him down. But Jack got right up and grabbed Ruddy and got an awful grip on him. "He's goin' to choke him now. He'll get him now, sure." And they tusseled for a while, Jack tryin' to get Ruddy's throat, but Ruddy always keepin' away, though pretty near gettin' it. Finally Ruddy broke clear loose and hit Jack an awful blow right in the chest. Then Jack went crazy mad. He rushed on Ruddy and got him by the throat and began to choke him. Meanwhile Ruddy was fightin' Jack's hands away and finally slipped 'em off again and as Jack came for him, Ruddy hit him and knocked Jack down again. Then he rushed on Jack and was about to choke him too, but Jack hopped up and kind of run off a little, then turned around and made for Ruddy again and struck Ruddy and knocked him into a heap. This was the first time for Ruddy; and he got right up and as Jack came up, he just rained the blows on Jack until Jack began to wilt and finally he came up with a regular sledge hammer and Jack fell over on the sand flat on his back, and lay there, his big white chest just goin' up and down like a bellows. I forgot to say that Harold Carman was there; and every time one was knocked down, he began to count. Mitch said if they counted 25 and you didn't get up, you was whipped. Well, this time Harold Carman counted 25 and then went on and counted 50 and still Jack didn't get up, but lay there his breast goin' up and down for air. Then everybody began to laugh. And the fight was given to Ruddy Hedgpeth; and when it was, Jack got up and picked up a club and started for Ruddy to kill him. So all the men pitched on to

Jack and began to hold him; and Jack was bloody and was swearin' and sayin' he had been tricked and that he could lick Ruddy with one hand in a fair fight. "Ruddy Hedgpeth is a coward," says Jack; "he put sweet oil on his chest and throat so I couldn't choke him when I got my hands on him. He's a coward and I've been tricked."

My pa was not a very big man, but he warn't afraid of no one. And he says: "Anything was fair, so as to whip, and you're whipped and you'd better shut up." So Jack made for my pa and pa stooped down and picked up a rock and stood his ground. The other men interfered; and George Montgomery said the sweet oil was fair and they all turned on Jack and he had to take his medicine. Then they broke up and started to climb the bank; and Mitch and me ran into the woods at the side of the road and waited until they went.

"How was that?" said Mitch.

"That was wonderful," says I.

"Well, you stick with me, and I'll show you a lot of things. Do you want to dig for treasure with me?" I said, "Of course"; and Mitch says: "We'll begin right away in Montgomery's woods. For I've been over there lots, and there are sloughs of dead limbs and we're bound to find it. I've got something on to-night. Mr. Bennett's daughter Nellie is goin' to be married and we can get under the window and see it. It's the grandest thing ever happened here. The wedding cake has diamonds on it, and everybody that comes, that's invited, of course, is given some kind of a gift, and Nellie has solid silver buckles on her shoes and a veil that cost $50. I'll come for you," says Mitch. And so a little after supper Mitch whistled for me, and we went to the Bennett house and fooled around waiting.

CHAPTER II

NOW Mr. Bennett had traded his farm for a store in town and was now a merchant prince, my pa said. And he had built him a wonderful stone house on a hill with a big yard around it. There was a house there before, and of course lots of trees, bushes around, and walks; and he had built a fine barn with lightning rods all over it with silver balls that just glittered. And he had a span of horses that cost $1000 and a wonderful carriage. He was awful rich. And Nellie was goin' to marry a man which was from Chicago. Pa and ma were goin' to the wedding; and ma could hardly get ready it took her so long to dress. She wore her silk dress which her sister had given her, and looked prettier than I ever saw her. Mitch and me had to sneak off because I was supposed to stay with Myrtle and Little Billie, as Delia, our girl, wanted to go out. Because I went, Delia had to stay, and she was as mad as hops.

But on the way over to Mr. Bennett's, Mitch told me that they had brought colored waiters from Chicago, from the Palmer House, the finest hotel in the world, where they had silver dollars in the floor. I couldn't believe this, but he said he had talked to Harold Carman, who had seen 'em with his own eyes, and counted 'em till he got tired. Mitch said that they had an orchestra from Chicago and were goin' to dance, that the wedding would cost $5000 which Mr. Bennett had offered to Nellie in money, or to take it for the cost of the wedding; and she took it for the wedding.

We climbed over the picket fence near the barn and dodged around past the bushes until we got up to a window where we kind of scrouched down and looked through lace curtains. There we saw everybody — all dressed up and talkin' and laughin'; and there was my pa and ma. Ma was holdin' her fan and talkin' to a man in a long black coat with all his white shirt showin', and diamonds in the shirt and a white tie. She looked very smilin' and different than when she talked to pa. Mitch's pa and ma warn't there, not bein' invited. The orchestra was playin' wonderful music; and finally all the people quit talkin'; the room got still, and the orchestra began to play somethin' very beautiful; and pretty soon Nellie Bennett came in holdin' the arm of Mr. Bennett, all in her veil and white satin, but I couldn't see the buckles on her shoes. And then the man she was goin' to marry — his name was Richard Hedges from Chicago — stepped out, and they both stepped in front of the minister, who was from Jacksonville, wearin' a black robe with white sash around his neck; and the orchestra stopped playin'. But just then we heard a twig or somethin' snap and we looked around quick and there was Doc Lyon who read the Bible all the time and acted queer. My pa thought he was crazy. And he began to say: "She doted on her lovers, on the Assyrians, her neighbors, which were clothed with blue, governors and rulers, all of them desirable young men, horsemen riding upon horses. I will take away thy nose and thy ears; and thy residue shall fall by the sword. They shall also strip thee of thy clothes and take away thy fair jewels."

Doc Lyon's voice sounded like he was talkin' out of
a cistern, and I grew sick at my stomach I was so scared.
But both Mitch and me forgot the wedding for the time
and turned our heads. And pretty soon we saw Doc
Lyon kind of rolling a pistol over in his hand. We could
see it. It glittered in the light; but Mitch and me were
lyin' in the shadow there, and I don't believe he knew
we were there. At least until I kind of lost my balance
and fell over against Mitch and bumped him against
the house, makin' a noise. We were scared to death,
for we was afraid Doc Lyon could now see us, and know
us, and would come over to us, and do something to us.
Everybody was afraid of him, especially the boys. Well,
probably he didn't know who it was, or but what maybe
it was a big dog. So he stood a minute and then began
to back off and finally turned and ran away into the
darkness. Then we looked in again, and by now the
minister was readin' from a book; and finally Mr.
Hedges put a ring on Nellie's finger; then they knelt
down and the minister prayed. Then they got up and
kissed and the music started; and everybody stood in
line to shake Nellie's hand and Mr. Hedges' hand, and
kiss Nellie. And there was a lot of talk and laughin'
and they began to dance. And Mitch whispered to me
we'd better go; that we'd seen it and we could get to
my house so as to let Delia go out and maybe square
everything. So we took a different way from what Doc
Lyon did, and ran as fast as we could, lookin' out for
corners we turned, and got home. Delia was awful
mad; it was about 9 o'clock now and she couldn't go
out. She said this wedding was no wedding anyway;
that Nellie Bennett was a heathen, havin' never been
baptized and that people that got married without bein'

baptized committed a sin. She was mad; but we edged around her, and finally she made some butter scotch for us and promised not to tell on us; and so did Myrtle and Little Billie.

Then Mitch and me began to talk about Doc Lyon and whether I shouldn't tell my pa so as to have him arrested; that he was a dangerous character. But how could I tell him without lettin' him know that we had been to the weddin', and our havin' Delia fixed? Then Mitch thought if we told and got my pa to arrest Doc Lyon and he got out, he would come for us, or maybe do somethin' to my pa. Anyhow Myrtle broke her word and told; but pa didn't say nothin' or do nothin'; he didn't talk much sometimes and nobody knew what he was thinkin' about.

Well, finally, Delia took Myrtle and Little Billie up to bed, and Mitch began to ask me if I knew about marriage. I had never seen anybody married before, but I knew about it because when I was only 6, the first day I went to school, a boy told me all about it, and it made me so shamed I didn't know what to do. And I didn't believe it; and when I told my ma, she said not to let boys tell me dirty lies, and to walk away from 'em. But since that time I had thought about it, and heard other things. I had heard my pa and ma say that Mrs. Rainey was in love with Temple Scott and wanted to marry him, although already married to Joe Rainey, her husband; and then you saw a lot of writin' on fences and sidewalks and on the schoolhouse walls; and some of the girls and boys said funny things sometimes. All the time it was plain enough that there couldn't be a family without a father as well as a mother; the father havin' to earn money, and the mother havin'

c

to take care of the children, and of course no children
where there were no father and mother, except orphans
and things like that.   Mitch and me talked this over and
he said that if any boy said any dirty thing to me, to hit
him one; and that if I'd come up some night, his pa
would explain to me about flowers and plants and show me
what a wonderful thing flowers are and how they mean
everything when understood. And then he began to talk
of Zueline Hasson, and how she made him feel so happy
and so in love with everything, just because she was so
beautiful, and her friendship was so beautiful to him.

Then Mitch wanted to know if I'd heard that this Mr.
Hedges was marryin' Nellie Bennett for her money,
and had come down from Chicago to get her for her pa's
money. I had heard my pa say that; and Mitch said, "I
believe it — there was too much splurge over there, and
why wasn't some man right here in this town good enough
for Nellie?" After a while pa and ma came home, and
Mitch hearin' 'em slipped out, and I was up-stairs by
the time they came up, with my light out. So I heard
pa and ma talk in the next room.

Pa said: "Yep, you'll see it before six months. Mr.
Bennett don't know any more about runnin' a store
than the man who got his farm knows about runnin' a
farm, which is nothin'. When men change their game,
this way, they always lose. And that ain't all. Mr.
Bennett is topplin' now. His house is mortgaged and
he's hard up. But a fine house is always a bait to young
men; and old folks always put out a bait in order to
marry their daughters off."

Ma said: "Nothin' of the kind. They don't have
to put out any bait. Look at you — was there any
bait about me?"

"No," says pa.

"Of course there wasn't," said ma. "And you went around sayin' it would kill you if I didn't marry you — and besides I have your letters for it."

"Oh, well," says pa, "a fellow always does that."

"Yes," ma said, "you're right, a fellow always does that, bait or no bait. And I think the way you talk about marriage sometimes is just awful, and if the children heard you, you'd be raisin' up children that suspicions marriage and every holy thing." And she went on to say that there was something wrong with pa and with lots of men, who went around cryin' and pretendin' to die, and then after they got the girl, talked about baits, and about bein' fooled.

And pa said: "Do you know what a woman is?"

And ma said: "I don't know what you think she is."

"A woman," says pa, "is a bottle of wine. If you look at it and leave it alone, never open it, the wine is as harmless as water. And if you leave a woman alone, she can't do nothin' to you. She's just there on the table or the shelf — harmless and just a woman, just like the bottle of wine is just a bottle of wine. But if you get in love with her, that's like drinkin' the wine; she gets hold of you, and you begin to talk and tell your secrets, and make promises, and give your money away, just like a drunk man. Then if you marry her, that's like getting over the wine; you wake up and find you've been drunk and you wonder what you've said, and if you remember, you smile at yourself, and your wife throws up to you what you said and that you wrote her letters. And the man who put wine, women and song together, put three things that was just the same together."

And ma says: "No, a woman ain't a bottle of wine at all; a woman is a bird."

"What kind?" says pa.

And ma says: "I don't know the name of the bird, but it roosts on the back of the hippopotamus. The hippopotamus is big and clumsy like a man and can't see very well, just like a man, and has lots of enemies like a man; so when enemies come this here bird sets up an awful clatter and squawkin' and that warns the hippopotamus and so he can run or defend himself. And if it wasn't for women, men couldn't get along, because they have to be warned and told things all the time, and given pointers what to do and how to act, and what is goin' on around — and the fact is women is brains, and men is just muscle."

And pa says, "How does this bird live, if it's on the back of the hippopotamus all the time?" That kind of got ma, for she knew if the bird got off the back of the hippopotamus to eat, it couldn't warn the hippopotamus, and as the bird has to live, ma was kind of stumped, and she says — "Oh, well the bird lives all right, it catches things that flies by."

"It does?" says pa. "You don't know your botany — that bird feeds off of the delicious insects that is on the back of the hippopotamus. So it don't have to get off for food, the same as a woman. And that ain't all," says pa; "men are performers and women is the audience; and women just sit and look and criticize, or maybe applaud if they like the performer; and men have to act their best, write the best books, and make the best speeches, and get the most money so as to please women which is the audience — and a woman can't do nothin' but applaud or criticize, and stir up the men to do their best — just because men, until they know better, want to please the women so as to get them for wives or somethin'."

And so pa went on till ma said: "I've heard enough of this —" and she went into the next room and slept with Little Billie.

And pa called out and said, "You ain't mad, are you?" And ma called back, "Just keep to your own self and shut up."

But as I can't come back to this again, I'll say that Mr. Bennett did fail and lose everything; and in about a year Nellie came back, her husband havin' left her after her pa failed; and she began to clerk in one of the stores, and is yet.

CHAPTER III

AFTER I met Mitch and after we saw the fight and the wedding, we went out to Montgomery's woods a few times in the afternoon when school was over. But we couldn't do much, because first we read "Tom Sawyer" along settin' on stumps and logs. We had to get the idea into our heads better; at least I did, because now we was about to carry out what Tom had done and wrote about — or what Mark Twain had wrote about for him. So we'd no sooner dig a few spadefuls than it would be gettin' dark, and we'd have to go home.

SITTING ON LOGS

One evening it began to rain and then thunder and lightnin', and we stood in a kind of shed for a bit, when all of a sudden I felt creepy and tingly, and saw a flash, followed by awful thunder; and of course I knew I had got a shock. Perry Strickland had been killed the summer before just this a way; and it seemed like once in a while God just launched out like you'd swat a fly, and took somebody; and of course you couldn't tell who He was goin' to come after next. Things like this, besides lots of other things, my grandpa's prayers and other things, had made me think a lot of religion, so as to be ready if I was to be took by lightnin' or drownin' or anything suddent. And some of the boys said that if you was drowned and didn't have nothin'

ALMOST STRUCK

on, you'd be kept out of heaven, and sent to a place of punishment. So it began to look like they was a lot of things to think about and be careful of.

I hadn't told Mitch because I didn't know just how he'd take it, even if he was a preacher's son; but I'd been goin' at nights sometimes down at a revival or protracted meeting at the church, not Mr. Miller's, but another church, a Baptist, I believe, or maybe Campbellite. And I had listened to the revivalist and heard the singin' and the experience speeches. And heard the revivalist say that you had to be immersed, that baptized meant to be put clear under, and that sprinklin' wouldn't do.

So I got Mitch to go the next night after the wedding, to see what he thought, but also to pay him back a little for takin' me to the fight and to the wedding. We went in together and sat down pretty fur back, and the meeting began. A man got up pretty fat and good natured, with a voice that just went into you like when you push one key of the organ down and keep pumpin'. And he said a long prayer and asked for light and help, and for light to shine in the hearts of the people present, so as to show 'em their sin; and to save people from death, and from sudden death, and if they died, then that they might be ready and be saved, And he asked for power to preach the gospel and for humbleness and understanding to receive the gospel after it was preached. And so on for a good while. And a good many said, "Amen." And then they sang "Angel Voices Ever Singing." Then the revivalist asked for songs and somebody called out, "Away in a Manger, No Crib for a Bed"; and they sang that. He asked for another one — and somebody called out, "There Were Ninety and Nine that Safely Lay." And somebody else wanted "I was a Wandering Sheep." And so it went till you could kind of feel things workin' up like when the lightning made me tingle. Then this revivalist preached a bit and talked about salvation and baptism, and about believin' and being baptized in order to be saved. Then they had another song, "Work, for the Night is Coming"; and then the revivalist called for experience speeches. And old John Doud, the photographer, got up first,

right away. He was bald and one of his eyes was out;
he was fat and his mouth watered. And he began to
tell what religion had done for him; how before he
got religion nobody could live with him, he was so selfish
and cross; how he was mean
to his wife, and how he drank
sometimes. And now he was all
different; he was happy all the
day and agreeable to everybody
and had been good to his wife
before she died, and generous
to everybody and didn't care
whether he had a dollar in his
pocket or a coat on his back so
long as he could help somebody;
and how he hated drink now —
couldn't bear the sight of it;
and he was thankful and ready
to die any minute and go to the
blest in heaven and meet his
wife, who was there. Lots of
people talked right out loud

JOHN DOUD

while he was speakin' and said, "Yes," "That's it,"
"That's what it does for you," and such like. And
he sat down, but popped right up again and said there
was a man in town who needed the prayers of the church
and he says, "You all know him — Joe Pink." Of course
we all knew Joe Pink, who was the honorariest man in
town, and a good deal in jail.

Then Harry Bailey got up. He'd had religion before
several times. Every winter he got it if there was a
revival; and if somebody had a new way of being baptized, he'd try it. He went on to say that he'd been

sprinkled and dipped; that he'd had the double baptism of bein' sprinkled and dipped, but he'd never been
really immersed — baptized; and now he knew it was
the only thing and he'd been livin' in sin all these years.
They said halleluyah to that, and everybody began to
shake his hand, and pat him on the back, till pretty
soon he keeled over in a fit like
he had sometimes, and the revivalist said — " Just stand back —
he may have the gift of tongues
and begin to prophesy." But
Harry just laid there kind a
kickin' like a chicken with its
head off and finally got up and
sat down ready to be received
into the church when they had
the general baptism. They had a
kind of tank under the pulpit, and
when they got enough to make it
worth while, the revivalist put on
rubber boots and stepped down
into this here tank and received
'em as they came to him, puttin'
'em clear under and then takin'
'em out.

MRS. PENNY

After Harry Bailey talked,
Mrs. Penny talked. She said
she could do more washin' since she got into the
church than ever, and that it had been the makin' of
her. John Cruzan, a fighter, said he hadn't wanted to
hurt a livin' soul since he was baptized. And so it went.

Mitch was settin' on the end of the seat next the aisle,
and I was on the inside. Pretty soon the revivalist

came down and spied Mitch. He just saw him as a boy, and didn't know who he was. Just then they were singin' "Knockin', Knockin', Who is There?" And it was dreadful solemn, some were moaning, others crying out, some were clappin' their hands, and lots were being

"ARE YOU SAVED, MY LITTLE FRIEND?"

talked to to bring 'em over. So this revivalist kneeled down and says to Mitch:

"Are you saved, my little friend?"

Mitch says, "Maybe, I don't know."

"Maybe," says he. "Well, don't you want to be certain to escape the condemnation?"

"I'd like to," says Mitch.

"This is the accepted time, and you can't afford to say maybe, you must say I am sure — I know it. What is your name?"

"Mitch Miller."

"Well, Mitch, have you had the advantages of a Bible training?"

"Yes, sir."

"You've read it a little?"

"All of it."

"Do you believe it?"

"Yes, sir."

"Well, then, why don't you stand up right now and say I believe it and come into the church?"

"I'd like to hear more about it."

"What part of it?"

"Baptism."

"There's nothing more to say, Mitch. The Bible says believe and be baptized. Baptized means to be immersed. The Bible doesn't say believe and be sprinkled, or believe and be dipped. It says believe and be baptized. You have it plain, and the duty is plain. You can come in now while you are young and before the grasshopper is a burden, or you can wait until the days of sin come about you, and your eyes are blinded with scales and then try to come in. And maybe by that time you will have lost interest and be hardened; or you may die in sin while saying 'maybe' and not 'I'm sure.' Now what do you say?"

And Mitch says, "I won't to-night anyway."

Then the revivalist said, "Do you remember the rich man to whom the Lord said, 'Thou fool, this night thy soul shall be required of thee'?"

Mitch says, "Yes, he was braggin' about his barns and that he had food laid up for many days. I'm not braggin' about anything; I'm not rich or grown up, and that part of the Bible don't apply to me."

"Ah," said the revivalist, just like that, "it all applies to you and to me — and it's Satan that tells it doesn't; and here you are a bright boy that has read the Bible and you hesitate and argue while Jesus is waitin'. But the time will come when Jesus won't wait — when the gates will be shut. And Jesus will be in heaven with His own, and all the rest will be in the pit, burning with eternal fire. Don't you believe this?"

Mitch says, "No."

"Then you don't believe the Bible. Who have you heard talk these subjects?"

"My pa."

"What does he do, Mitchie?"

"He's a preacher."

The revivalist was stunned, and he looked at Mitch and kind of started to get away from him. Then Mitch says: "My pa debated baptism with another preacher last winter and beat him. I believe in sprinklin'. I've been sprinkled, and I will let it stay that way until I'm convinced."

Then the revivalist says: "Take your chance, my little friend," and went away. The meeting ended and we went home. To-morrow was Saturday, and we were going to dig for treasure.

CHAPTER IV

MITCH and I had dug under pretty near every dead limb in Montgomery's woods and hadn't found a trace of any treasure. We began in April when the winds sang as they did in March. There were black-birds around then and that bird that sings "spring day." Mitch's father knew the names of all the birds; but outside of crows, robins, jay-birds and things like that we didn't know 'em — neither Mitch nor I. We didn't care, for what's the use of knowing names of things? You can't pronounce 'em anyway, and I've noticed people get queer studying such things, like Homer Jones who gathered weeds and flowers and pinned long names on 'em.

When we began to dig, the sap was flowing out of the maple trees. And once George Montgomery saw us digging. He had come over to empty his buckets of sap to make some maple sugar. And he said, "What are you boys doing?" and laughed and said — "Don't bother my buckets. If you want a taste of sap take it, but don't get the buckets askew so they will spill."

Mitch called back to him, "What do you say, George, if we find a tea-kettle of money buried here sommers, buried by old Nancy Allen?" And George said, "Take it along — but you'll dig the whole world up before you do."

You see Mitch was foolin' because we didn't think Nancy Allen had left her money there, if she had any.

But Mitch didn't want to say that we was followin' the direction of Tom Sawyer for treasure. We kept the book hid under a log, and every now and then would take it out and read it to see if we missed any of the points.

If we had told George Montgomery what we was doin', he would have laughed at us and told everybody, and had the whole town laughin' at us. Because we knew nobody but us had any faith in such things. But Mitch had faith and so had I. We agreed that there was treasure to be found, and if we worked we believed we could get it.

It was a good thing that Nancy Allen died that winter and that Mitch said that, be-

GEORGE MONTGOMERY

cause it threw George off. Nobody believed in Tom Sawyer as a real person but us — we did. We knew he was real. Mitch was going to write a letter to him and send it to Hannibal, Missouri, for Mitch's dad said there was no town of St. Petersburg in Missouri — and that Mark Twain had used that name as a blind.

And just about then this here Nancy Allen disappeared. She was a funny little woman about as big as a 'leven year old girl, and wore a shawl around her head, and carried a cane and smoked a pipe. She allus came to town with Old Bender and his wife which was a friend or somethin' of Nancy, and a boy with a mouth as big as a colt's and as trembly, which was Old Bender's boy. They all lived together near town, and used to come in, first Old Bender, then his wife, then Nancy, then this boy walkin' in file, and they'd go to the grocery store

THE BENDER FAMILY

and set around all day, and go home with bacon, tobacco and things.

I said Nancy disappeared in the winter. But there was snow and they didn't come to town — so just when she died nobody knows. But as I said, Mitch and I found her body right near a creek in Montgomery's woods in April. The snow was gone, and there she lay, what was left of her, wrapped up in her shawl. And no one knew how she got there or anything about it.

Mitch was the most curious boy you ever saw. He

had read sommers about a singing bone — that if you
take the bone of a person that has died like this, and
hollow it out so as to make it into kind of a horn, and
blow through it, a voice will come out of it and tell you
how the person died and where the money is that's left
and everything. So when we found her, Mitch was
just about to take her arm bone which was stickin'
through her shawl to make a horn of when I says, "Don't,
Mitch, you'll get into trouble. That body must lie
right there 'till the Corner comes." You see my father
was States Attorney and I'd heard him say that. So
we left Nancy just as she was and ran into town. I told
my father, and the Corner went out and took us along,
and we told what we knew. Then they took her body
into town and got a jury and Mitch and I told about it,
and our names were printed in the paper.

There was a story around that Nancy Allen was a
miser, and of course they wondered how she died. And
my pa got Old Bender in and cross-questioned him a
whole day, with Mitch and me hid on top of a closet
in the room. But Old Bender stuck to his story, that
Nancy had started out to visit one of the Watkinses
near Montgomery's woods, and probably got cold, or
fainted or somethin'. Anyway, they let Old Bender
go, and after that he came into town walkin' first, then
his wife, then their boy, and Nancy gone.

They didn't find any money or anything. But George
Montgomery was threw clean off when Mitch said we're
diggin' for Nancy's treasure. For Mitch went on and
said : "What was she doin' here in the woods? Goin'
to see the Watkinses? That's pretty thin. She was
here to get her money, that's what it was. And she
fainted and froze to death. It's as plain as day. My pa

D

thinks so, and that ain't all, the States Attorney thinks
so too, doesn't he, Skeeters?" Of course I had to say
yes, though I'd never heard my pa say any such thing.
George left us and went about his buckets, and we went
on diggin'. We saw George walk away and climb the
rail fence and disappear. Then Mitch flung down his
spade and sat on the log where we had "Tom Sawyer"
hid and began to talk.

"Skeeters," he said, "just look how everything
tallies. Tom's town was St. Petersburg, and ours here
is Petersburg. His town was on a river. So is this
town. We ain't got no Injun Joe, but how about Doc
Lyon? Ain't he just as mysterious and dangerous as
Injun Joe? Then if these woods don't look just like the
woods Tom and Huck dug in, I'll eat my hat. Look
here!" Mitch pulled the book out and showed me, and
sure enough they were alike. "Then look at Old Taylor,
the school teacher — ain't he the livin' image of Tom's
teacher? And our schoolhouses look alike. And we
ain't got any Aunt Polly, but look at your grandmother
— she's the livin' image of Aunt Polly and just like her.
Things can't be just alike, if they was, they wouldn't be
two things, but only one. And I can go through this
town and pick out every character. I've thought it
over. The Welshman — that's George Montgomery's
father. Nigger Jim — how about Nigger Dick? He's
older and drinks, but you must expect some differences.
And Mary — my sister Anne is just the same. Muff
Potter — how about Joe Pink? — allus in trouble and in
jail and looks like Muff. And the Sunday School's
just the same, superintendent and all. And the circus
comes to town just as it did in Tom's town. And the
County Judge — no difference."

"Yes, but," I said, "your girl ain't the daughter of the County Judge like Becky Thatcher was. And her name is Zueline and that sounds like something beautiful not belonging to any town — but to some place I keep dreaming about."

"Skeeters," said Mitch, " you make me mad sometimes. As I told you, it can't be all alike. Now there's you — you ain't any more like Huckleberry Finn than the Sunday School superintendent is, not sayin' that you're him, for you're not. But it can't be all alike. I only say when it goes this far that it means something. And while I think I'm just like Tom Sawyer, for I can do everything he did, swim, fight, fish and hook sugar, and read detective stories, you're not Huck, and because you're not, it will be different in the end. We'll go along up to a certain point, and then it will be you, maybe, that'll give it a different turn. Maybe we'll get bigger treasure or somethin' better."

"I don't want no better luck than Tom and Huck had," said I. "But I believe it will be different, for you're different from Tom, Mitch. For one thing, you've read different things: The Arabian Nights, and Grimm's Stories, and there's your father who's a preacher and all your sisters and your mother who's so good natured and fat. These things will count too. So I say, if I'm not Huck, you're not Tom, though we can go on for treasure, and I see your argument mostly and believe in it."

Mitch grew awful serious and was still for a long while. Finally he said : "Skeeters, I just live Tom Sawyer and dream about him. I don't seem to think of anything else — and somehow I act him, and before I die, I mean to see him. Yes, sir, this very summer you and I, if

you're game, will look on Tom Sawyer's face and take
him by the hand."

"Why, Mitch," I said, "how can you do it? It must
be more'n a hundred miles from here to where Tom
lives."

"You bet it is," said Mitch. "It's near two hundred
miles. I looked it up. But it's as easy as pie to get there.
Look here — we can bum our way or walk to Havaner
— then we can get a job on a steamboat and go to St.
Louis — then we can bum or walk our way to Hannibal
— and some fine mornin' you and I will be standin' on
the shore of the Mississippi — and there'll be Tom and
Huck, and you and me. And I'll say, 'Tom Sawyer,
I'm Mitch Miller, and this here is Skeeters Kirby.'
How's that for fun? Just think of it. I dream about
this every night. And we'll strip and go swimmin',
and fish and all go up to McDougal's Cave. And what
would you say if we persuaded them to come back with
us for a visit? Tom and Huck, you and me all walkin'
arm in arm down the streets here? Why, the town'd
go wild. And we'd go out to your grandmother's and
stay all summer and just roll in pie and cake and good
things — and ride horses, and fly kites. My — I just
can't wait!"

So Mitch went on this way for quite a spell and then
he switched and said: "Skeeters, what do you dream
about?" "Flyin'," says I. "No!" said Mitch. "Do
you really?" "As sure as you're livin'," I says. "Well,
ain't that funny," said Mitch, "so do I. But how do
you do it, with wings or how?" "No," I says, "I
seem to reach up my hands and pull myself up, by
rounds on a ladder, ropes or somethin'; and I'm always
trying to get away from somethin' — like bears or some-

times it's a lion. But pa says it means I'm an aspirin' nature and born to pull up in the world. But," says I to Mitch, "do you ever dream of the Judgment Day?"

"Do I?" says Mitch. "You can better believe I do — and that's where my flyin' comes in, only I drift like one of these here prairie chickens about to light — I seem to be goin' down. And it was just last night I dreamed of the Judgment Day. First everything was mixed : here was Injun Joe and Doc Lyon, Joe Pink and Muff Potter, Aunt Polly and your grandma — every-

body in these two towns all together. And Tom Sawyer, Huck Finn, Joe Harper, Becky, Zue-line, and your folks and mine — all of us was together. And then suddenly we seemed to be close to Bucky Gum's pas-ture; the well became a kind of pipe stuck up out of the ground and began to spout fire; and there was a great light in the

THE JUDGMENT DAY

sky and I saw Jesus coming down out of the sky, and there was thunder. Then I began to fly — drift down, and all of a sudden, kerplunk, I fell out of bed. And pa says — 'Hey, Mitch, what's the matter?' 'It's the Judgment Day,' I says. 'Judgment nothin', says pa — 'You've fallen out of bed. Get back in bed and go to

sleep — you were hollerin' like an Indian.' Then I
heard ma say to pa after a bit, 'Pa, you oughtn't to
read so much of the Bible before the children. It makes
'em nervous.' Now, Skeeters, what do you dream about
the Judgment Day?"

I was just about to tell him when I heard some one
comin'. I looked up. It was Kit O'Brien and Mike
Kelly comin' from the slaughter house. They had some

WHIPPING KIT O'BRIEN

liver and a bladder; and before we could square around
Kit O'Brien came up and knocked " Tom Sawyer " out of
Mitch's hand. And then it began. These boys belonged
to a gang over the hill back of where old Moody lived,
and we was always fightin'. Mitch and Kit had fit before
— and so had Mike and me. Mike licked me once and I
licked him once. But Mitch had given Kit an awful lickin'
with no come back. So now he thought his chance had
come with Mike to help after disposin' of me. So what
did they do, both of 'em, but go quick for Mitch, thinkin',
I guess, to get rid of him and then lick me.

"No, you don't," says I; and I grabbed both of Mike's arms with my arms and held him out for to wrestle. I was awful strong in the back and arms and rangy, and nobody could trip me, and I could back up until I got a feller comin' good and then give a swing and land him. So there we was at it — I holdin' Mike, and Mitch and Kit squared off boxin' like mad. I gave Mike the swing and tumbled him, and then lay on him and held him down. But it was awful hard and he was gradually gettin' away from me, and strikin' me in the chest and sometimes in the face. He had big fists and an awful punch. Meantime I was watchin' Mitch and Kit as much as I could and neither of 'em seemed to have much the best of it, when all of a sudden I heard a voice say, "Stop that," and there was Henry Hill, the town marshal, drivin' a lot of kids ahead of him. Well, we all stopped fightin'. And what do you suppose? Jerry Sharp who had a garden near Fillmore Creek had complained about the boys goin' in swimmin' where his girls settin' out tomato plants could see. So the marshal had come down and arrested 'em and was drivin' 'em into town.

He just added Mitch and me and Kit and Mike to the crowd and took us all in. When we got to the calaboose, he unlocked the door and started to put us in. Then he laughed and said, "Now go home." And so we hustled away.

CHAPTER V

IT warn't more'n a day or two after this that my pa said that Old Bender's house had burned down the night before, and he thought maybe the old feller had set it afire. You see the story still clung about Nancy Allen, and maybe he'd killed her, and my pa bein' the States Attorney started to look into it.

Mitch and me and Little Billie were sittin' on the steps listenin' to Mitch readin' "Tom Sawyer," and my sister was there too. She always seemed in the way somehow, because she looked so steady with big eyes and every now and then would ask questions that Mitch couldn't answer or no one. While we was sittin' there my pa drove up in a rig, and said he was drivin' out to Bender's house that was burned, and wanted ma to go. She couldn't, and so I spoke up and asked him to take Mitch and me, and he said get in. Then Little Billie began to cry to go — but pa said no, and I did. But when we got on the way, I saw tears in Mitch's eyes, and he said, "I'll never go again and leave Little Billie. It ain't fair and I can't stand it." Mitch was the tenderest hearted boy you ever see.

By and by we got out there, and sure enough the house was burned down, all fallen into the cellar. And Old Bender was pokin' around, and his wife and the boy with the big mouth. Nigger Dick was there cleanin' things away. My pa had sent him out to do it. We

began to fuss around too and pa was askin' Old Bender
how the fire started and all that.

Well, sir, what do you suppose? I got down in the
cellar and began to scrape around and kick ashes and
sticks around; and all at
once I struck iron or
something, and I scraped
off the ashes and things
and there was a soap
kettle turned upside
down, and sunk like in
the dirt floor of the cellar. I leaned down and
tugged and pulled it up
and inside was a lot of
cans, four or five, and
inside the cans the greatest lot of money you ever
see. Great big copper
coins and silver dollars
and paper dollars. Well,
I was just paralyzed. I
couldn't believe my eyes.
Struck it, I says to my-
self — struck it without
any more trouble or
worry, and no need to see
Tom Sawyer and find out

NIGGER DICK

how to find treasure. Here it was before my eyes. After
a bit I called out, "O, Mitch" — but he was around
sommers and didn't come till I called again. Then he
peeked over into the cellar and I just pointed and
couldn't speak. Mitch slid down into the cellar and

bent over lookin' at the money, and turned to me and
said, "Well, Skeeters, this is all right for you — but not
for me. You found it, and I didn't. You've won out,
but I've got to go on and find some for my own self."

STRUCK IT, I SAYS

"Not on your life," says I. "What's mine is yours.
And besides we came here together — we've been working together; if we hadn't, you wouldn't have been
here, and I wouldn't. It's all because we've been chums

and huntin' together — and half of this is yours, just the same as half of it would be mine if you'd happened to get in the cellar first."

Just then Mitch found a piece of paper with Nancy Allen written on it, and a little bundle which he unwrapped and found inside a breast pin with the initials N. A. on it, which showed that the money was Nancy Allen's, saved from sellin' rags and paper. For we remembered when she used to go about with a gunny sack pickin' up old rags, bottles and things.

I was just puttin' the cans into the kettle when pa came up and saw me, and says, "What you got?" Then he saw what it was. And Nigger Dick came up and says, "Bless my soul!" And pa took the kettle up on the ground and began to count the money. "That's mine," I said to pa; but he didn't notice me, just went on countin' till he found out there was about $2000.00. Then he said, "This money goes to the county. Nancy Allen didn't have any relatives, and it goes to the county." Well, I began to perk up and I said, "Ain't Mrs. Bender her sister — and if it ain't mine for findin' it, why don't it go to her sister?" Pa said: "No, Mrs. Bender ain't her sister, and I know she didn't have any relatives. Anyway, we'll advertise and if no relatives claim the money, it goes to the county."

I began to sniffle. And Mitch says: "Tell me, then, how Tom Sawyer and Huck Finn got to keep what they found. Injun Joe had no relatives, and Judge Thatcher knew the law, or was supposed to; and why didn't that money go to the county?"

"Why, Mitch," said pa, "don't you know that's just a story? You don't take that for true. You mustn't let a yarn like that get into your head and fix your ideas about things. And it's a good lesson to both of you. You'll find when you grow up that there'll be lots of prizes that are just about to fall in your hands when some superior right takes 'em away. And you'll find that everything that happens in boyhood and on the school yard happens when you grow up, only on a bigger scale, and hurts more. And you'll see that everything in life when you're grown is just a repetition of what happens on the school yard — friendship, games, battles, politics, everything."

By this time Nigger Dick had come up again and he said he'd found some footprints coming to and going away from the house. It had rained the night before and the marks had staid. So pa got Old Bender and made him walk and compared the prints, but they wasn't the same. And pa said that was a clew. For Old Bender claimed he woke up and found the house on fire. So they took a box and turned it upside down over some of the prints and then pa took the kettle and put it in the rig, and Old Bender came up and said that he knew Nancy Allen had some money, but he didn't know where she kept it. Then we drove away.

Pa was quiet, like he was thinkin'. But I could see Mitch was mad, not that he expected any of the money, but because he wanted me to have it and thought I deserved it.

We drove past the Old Salem mill comin' home. We'd fished there lots of times, Mitch and I — not this summer yet, but other summers. We used to sit on the dam and fish. And pa hadn't hardly said a word till we came to the mill. Then he said, " If you boys are lookin' for treasure, why don't you come here?" He knew we'd been diggin' in Montgomery's woods, but didn't say

nothin'. Then Mitch says, "Where would you dig —
along the shore or where? Or is there a cave around
here?" Pa said "whoa" and stopped the horses. He said,
"Look up there. Don't that look like Cardiff's hill in
' Tom Sawyer'?" "Well, it does," said Mitch.

Here was a high hill hanging right over the road and
about twict as high as the mill, or maybe more, with a
road winding up to the top. And pa says: "More
treasure was found on the top of that hill than anywhere
in the world, and who knows, maybe some is left there
yet. Now I'm going to take Nancy Allen's money and
put it in my vault in the court house. You boys can't
have it. It's against the law. But I promise you that
any treasure you find here, I'll let you keep."

I felt better now, and Mitch's eyes were standin' out
of his head. Then pa said, "Get up" to the horse, and
we drove into Petersburg about a mile. Mitch tried to
get pa to say where it was best to dig; but pa said:
"You boys go out there — see what you can find, dig
around too, if you want to, and tell me what you find."

We got into town after a while and pa took the kettle
with all the cans out of the rig and we followed him
into his office and saw him put 'em into the vault and
close the door and turn the knob. It was worse than
buryin' a pet dog to see this. It took away our hopes.
But there was no help for it. So we walked out and Mitch
said, "If you'll come up to supper, I'll come back to
your house and stay all night." "That's a go," I said,
"And besides to-morrow is Saturday, and you promised
to help me make garden, if I'd help you." And Mitch
said all right, and so we went to his house.

The Miller family was awful big, five girls and Mitch,
and all the healthiest children you ever saw, fat and rosy

and full of fun ; and we had the best times there you ever knew of. And Mr. Miller was always reading to Mrs. Miller, with all the children racin' through the house and laughin'. It made no difference — he read right on ; but sometimes Mrs. Miller would look up from her sewin' and say, " Read that over, Robert, I lost that," and that would be when the children made such a noise you couldn't hear nothin'. So when we got to the house, there was Mr. Miller, readin' English history to Mrs. Miller, and the children already playin' blind man's buff, and makin' a terrible noise, though it was before supper. Zueline Hasson had come over and was goin' to stay to supper too. She was Angela Miller's friend besides bein' Mitch's sweetheart. You ought to have seen Mitch look when he saw Zueline. He just stood a minute like he was lookin' at an angel he was afraid of.

Pretty soon Mrs. Miller said she had to have a bucket of water, and Mitch went to pump it, and Zueline went with him. The sun was down now, but it was bright day, and the robins were singin' their heads off, and the air smelt of grass and flowers. I stood at the kitchen window and watched Mitch pump a cup of water for Zueline and hand it to her. And I knew what it meant ; for Mitch had told me that he couldn't be near her without a lump comin' into his throat. He said it was like religion, for Mitch had got religion too, and he'd seen lots of people get it, and he knew what it was. And as for Zueline, she thought Mitch was the finest boy in town, which he was.

By and by we set down to supper. There was nine of us, and the awfullest gigglin' and talkin' you ever heard, even before Mr. Miller had hardly finished sayin' grace. We had oatmeal and eggs and biscuits and jam

and milk; and Mr. Miller was talkin' English history
to Mrs. Miller, no more disturbed by us children than if
we wasn't there. After that we played blind man's
buff. And every time Mitch could find Zueline, and

MITCH PUMPS A CUP OF WATER

trace her about the room, though she didn't make any
noise at all, and I knew he couldn't see. It was almost
spooky.

Before we started to go Mitch said he had to feed
Fanny, which was his dog that he loved most to death.

Fanny was about to have some puppies, and he kept
her in the barn. So we made up a dish of things and went
out to the barn, Mitch whistlin' all the way and callin'
to her. "That's funny," said Mitch. "She doesn't
answer. I wonder why." We got to the barn and
opened the door and he called again, but no Fanny.
Then he went in and tramped around the stalls but

couldn't find her. So
Mitch went back to the
house for a lantern and
we looked all through the
barn and finally all
around the barn. And
pretty soon he saw her
lyin' by the barn. She
was dead—all over blood.
Somebody had run a great
knife like a scythe or a
corn-cutter through her.
And I never see a boy
cry like Mitch did. He
ran back and told Zueline
and she and all the chil-
dren came out and most

CRYING FOR FANNY

of us cried. Then Mr. Miller came out, and Mrs. Miller,
and Mr. Miller said he believed Doc Lyon had done it
— that he had seen him in the alley in the afternoon.
And Mitch said he'd kill Doc Lyon. And that scared
Mrs. Miller, and she said, "Keep away from him,
Mitchie, he's gone crazy over religion and he'll kill you."
"It's a good day," said Mitch, "Skeet loses his treasure,
and my dog's killed — it's a good day." Then Zueline
took Mitch's hand and said, "Never mind, my pa's goin'

to get me an Ayrdale and I'll make him get two, one for you." So we threw a blanket over Fanny and Mitch took Zueline home, and I went home and waited for Mitch to come.

When he did come he was in better spirits. Zueline had cheered him up. He said he worshiped her — that he'd kill any one who spoke a bad word about her, and that he intended to protect her as long as he lived.

Then Mitch and me went to my house. It was now about ten o'clock, and pa hadn't come home. There seemed to be a lot stirrin' someway, and ma said, "Your father is very busy, and we'll all go to bed and not wait for him. He has a key of his own." So pretty soon we were all in bed with the lights out. And in about a minute we heard the latch in the stairway door begin to rattle, and ma says, "What's that?" and called down and said, "Is that you, pa?" No answer, just the rattlin'. Well, ma had bolted the door on the inside, and whoever it was couldn't open the door at once, but kept up the rattlin'. Then ma turned white and said, "One of you boys must go for George Montgomery. I'll let one of you out of the window and the other must stay here and help to fight." Mitch said, "You go, Skeet, you're a faster runner than me, and maybe he'll hop after you, whoever he is. I'll stay here and take a bed-slat and brain him as he comes up the stairway." "No," says I, "I think it's more dangerous to stay than to go — let's draw straws to see who goes." Meantime ma took a sheet off the bed. We drew straws and the lot fell to me to go. So ma let me down by the sheet. No sooner did I reach the ground than bang went the dining room window and the man was after me.

I went over the first fence like a deer, the man after

E

me. I ran up the road, took the back fence of Montgomery's place, and ran up the arbor way. I knew the
land, the feller after me didn't. I lost him somewhere.
In a minute I was under George's window, calling. He
was still up and he came right down with his walking

CATCHING DOC LYON

stick and a pistol, just as good natured and comfortin'
as he could be.

George went all through the house, but found no one.
Then we went to the barn, but found nothing. As we
were coming back, I saw some one drop down behind
the raspberry bushes. George saw it too, and made for
the fellow. He fired at us. The bullet whizzed past
Mitch's head, and we dropped in the grass. But George
went on, shooting as he went, and finally got up to the
fellow and struck his arm down as he was about to fire.
Then he grabbed him and took away his pistol. And
there was Doc Lyon!

CHAPTER VI

THE next morning Nigger Dick came to beat carpets, for ma was cleanin' house; and Mitch and me were makin' garden, and talkin' to Nigger Dick. He was the funniest nigger you ever saw and the best hearted, except when he was drunk, then he was cross and mumbled to himself. His wife was Dinah who wore circle ear-rings and used to cook for the Bransons when they had lots of company. The Bransons were the richest people in town and had lots of parrots and poodles, and Mrs. Branson et snuff. They was from Virginia, ma said; and Mitch and I used to talk to Dinah over the back fence when she was cookin' there. She wore a red bandanna around her head, and she used to say, "Look heah, you boys, if you see that nigger drinkin', you come and tell me, cuz I ain't goin' to live with him no more if he drinks." Then

DINAH

she'd hand us out cookies or somethin', and say go along.

Nigger Dick was singin':

> Nicodemus was a slave of African birth,
> Who was bought for a purse full of gold,

and beatin' carpets, and doin' whatever ma told him. She kept changing her mind and would say: "Here, Dick, help me with this picture. Now you can leave that and set out this geranium. Here, Dick, that can go for a while, go down to the barn and bring up that barrel there and put this stuff in it."

Dick knew ma, and bein' disorderly himself, didn't care what he did, or whether he finished anything. So he kept saying, "Yes'm," "Yes'm," and workin' away. So every time Dick got near us, we'd talk to him and get him to tell us about his father which was a slave, or about Kentucky. Little Billie was playin' near us, for Mitch was makin' him a little onion bed, and Dick was ridin' Little Billie on his shoulder, and he was as gay as a jay-bird and singin'. One of his songs was:

> Oh, said a wood-pecker settin' on a tree,
> I once courted a fair ladee.
> She proved fickle and from me fled,
> And ever since then my head's been red.

And "Babylon is Fallin'" was another of his songs, and "Angel Gabriel." Mitch would rather be around where Nigger Dick was than any one. He almost laughed himself sick that mornin'.

Well, we told Nigger Dick about catchin' Doc Lyon; and we took him around to where I had been let down by the sheet, and showed him how I had run and jumped the fence to get away. Nigger Dick began to act awful mysterious and say, "You can't fool this nigger," and he kept goin' back and forth from the window to the fence, lookin' at the ground. And by and by he went and asked ma if he could go down town. He wanted to see my pa about somethin'. So he went off, and Mitch and I went on makin' garden, till ma came and set us to work buildin' a flower bed. That was one trouble with ma, you no sooner got started on one thing than she changed her mind and wanted you to do somethin' else. "Never mind," said Mitch, "we're havin' fun, whatever it is. But what do you suppose your pa meant by sayin' that that hill above the Old Salem mill had given up more treasure than any place in the world? Who got it? Now pa says that Linkern lived there onct and kept store, but he didn't get it. He was so poor that he used to have welts on his legs from wearin' the same buckskin pants. That's what pa says. So if he didn't get the treasure, who did? It couldn't be Mr. Branson, for he got his start raisin' onions and peddlin' 'em here in town. All the same, your pa must have meant somethin'. But I tell you, Skeet, we've lost this Saturday, and it's too far to go after school. So I say let's go out there next Saturday — start early and prospect around as they say — look the land over. And keep goin' till we clean the place up, like we did Montgomery's woods."

Just then pa and Nigger Dick drove up. Pa had a shoe in his hand and went and began to put the shoe in the prints where Doc Lyon had run from the window to the fence. "It fits," says Dick, and laughed, and I said to pa, "What you got, Doc Lyon's shoe?" And pa said, kind of gruff and absent minded, "Yes." "Well," says I, "You don't need any shoe to tell it was Doc

Lyon that chased me." Pa didn't answer me. He said, "Come on, Dick," and they started for the buggy. Ma came runnin' to the door and said, "Where you goin', Dick? The carpets must be cleaned and laid." "I don't know," says Dick, "I'm in the hands of the law." "Back after while," said pa, as he gave the horse a tap with the whip and drove off.

Ma stood in the door and said : "No order, no system, never anything done. It's just too discouraging. Just as I get Dick and have him well started at work, your pa comes and takes him off." Then she turned to us and said, "Don't work any more on the flower bed. Come with me. I want you boys to build a chicken coop. The old hen must be shut up to-night, and you must hurry." Mitch smiled a little, but we went into the back yard and got some lath and made the coop.

Well, after while Nigger Dick came back. They had driven out to Bender's place and put the shoe in the foot-prints out there, and sure enough they fit and pa had gone to the jail and quizzed Doc Lyon about the fire and he had confessed and told everything. And that wasn't all. "Why," said Nigger Dick, "that Doc Lyon is the devil himself. He killed Nancy Allen — Yes, he did. He says so. And that ain't all. He killed your dog, Mitch. And even that ain't all; all these cows that got cut so they couldn't give milk, he cut 'em — yes sir, that devil cut 'em. And your pa is goin' to have him hanged. And that ain't all. If he'd got upstairs last night, he'd a killed your ma. Yes, sir. He's the awfulest devil in this county. And you see when he used to go to Sunday School and walk the streets readin' the Bible, he was just playin' possum. He'd sold himself to the devil and he was tryin' to hide it."

I said to Mitch, "Was Injun Joe ever in jail?" Mitch said: "Skeet, you don't act like sense sometimes. You know dern well he was in jail. How could he get into court if he wasn't in jail? Don't you remember when Tom was testifyin' agin him that he broke loose and jumped through the court house window and escaped, and nobody ever saw him again until Tom found his body at the door of McDougal's cave?"

"Well," says I, "he might have been out on bail." "What's that?" said Mitch. "I don't know," says I. "It's a way to keep from goin' to jail, and since the book don't say that Injun Joe was in jail, I'll bet you he never was. Poor old Muff Potter was in jail after the murder and he didn't kill anybody. It was Injun Joe that did the killin'. And don't you remember that Tom and Huck went to the jail one night and stood on each other's backs so they could talk to Muff through the bars?" "I have an idea," says Mitch, "let's go to the jail to-night and talk to Doc Lyon. Your pa and Jasper Rutledge, the sheriff, are friends, and he knows us. And besides, Joe Pink is in jail. Look at it: Joe Pink is Muff Potter and Doc Lyon is Injun Joe, and we'll go to see 'em just like Tom and Huck went to see Muff Potter. Only, as I said before, Skeet, you're no more like Huck than my pa is like Nigger Dick."

"Well," says I, "it makes no difference. We'll go. For you can bet Doc Lyon will never be free again, and we can look at him and ask him questions, and see what he has to say."

We got down to the jail about dusk, and Mitch insisted on rollin' a barl up to the window and climbin' up on it, so as to make it as much like Tom Sawyer as possible.

The window was too high for us to stand on each other's backs. Just as we got the barl up, along comes Jasper Rutledge, the sheriff, and he says, "Hey, what you boys doin'?" "We want to talk to Doc Lyon," says I. "What about?" says he. "About my dog," says Mitch. The sheriff looked at us curious for a minute and says, "If I let you talk to him, will you promise not to tease him or get him mad?" "Yes, Mr. Rutledge," both of us said. "Well then," said the sheriff, "don't fool around with that barl; I'll let you inside the jail and you can stand comfortable and talk to him." Mitch didn't know what to say to this. He just toed the ground with his toe, and finally said, "We'd rather stand on the barl, Mr. Rutledge." I knew what he meant. It wouldn't be like Tom Sawyer to go inside. And the sheriff laughed and said, "Well, I'll swan, have it your way. But mind you, I'm going to hide and hear what is said, for I want to hear what he says about all this devilish work. But if you tease him or say anything out of the way, I'll stop it and drive you off."

So we promised and Mitch rolled the barl up to the winder and we both stood on it and looked in. First thing we see was Joe Pink. He was in there for bein' drunk, and beatin' his wife. And he went on to tell about his life, how he'd most worked himself to death tryin' to support her and the children, and how she couldn't cook, and how she never had the meals ready, and how he'd come home so hungry he could eat glue, and she'd be talkin' over the back fence with Laura Bates, and how he didn't like her any more anyway, because she had lost most of her teeth, and spluttered her words. Then he'd get drunk, he said, to forget. And just then a voice said, "No drunkard shall enter the kingdom of heaven." It was Doc Lyon in a separate place, behind another iron door. And Joe Pink turned on him and said: "I suppose dog killers and house burners and cow-cutters and murderers get in. They **do,** do they? Well, you can send Joe Pink down to the devil. I don't want to go nowhere where you go — you can bet on that."

By this time we could see clear into the dark, and there stood Doc Lyon quiet like, his hands holding the bars, awful white hands, and his eyes bright like a snake's when it raises up to strike. Then Doc Lyon began to talk. First he was talking about Mitch's dog. He said it wasn't decent to have that dog around where children could see her, and that he had killed her because God told him to. Then he began to talk the Bible and talk about Ohalibah and say: "She doted on her lovers, on the Assyrians, her neighbors, which were clothed with blue, governors and rulers, all of them desirable young men, horsemen riding upon

DOC LYON

horses. And I will set my jealousy against thee, and they shall deal with thee in fury; they shall take away thy nose and thine ears; and thy residue shall fall by the sword. They shall also strip thee of thy clothes and take away thy fair jewels." And so he went on for a long time. And Mitch whispered to me, "He's quoting from Ezekiel" — Mitch had heard his pa read it to his ma and he knew it.

Then Doc Lyon went on to talk about my ma, and to say that he didn't mean to kill her, but only to cut off her ears and her nose, because she was too pretty, and was an abomination to the Lord because she was so pretty, and the Lord had told him to do it. And then he said the Lord had told him to remove Nancy Allen because she lived with Old Bender and his wife, and it wasn't right. He was awful crazy; for if ever there was a harmless old couple and a harmless old woman, it was the Benders and Nancy Allen. And why did he want to kill her for livin' with the Benders? She had to live sommers, and didn't have any home of her own.

We didn't have to say hardly a word — Doc Lyon just went on and told about settin' Bender's house on fire to purify the abomination of the dwelling, he said, where Nancy Allen had lived.

We heard enough and slid off the barl. Then Jasper Rutledge came out and said : "Can you boys remember what he said? For that's a free confession he made, and you must testify, and I will. There'll be a hangin' in this jail, before the snow flies."

I was so scared and shook up that I was afraid to sleep alone. So as we went by, I asked ma if I could stay all night with Mitch. She said "yes." So when we got to Mitch's home, Mr. Miller was readin' to Mrs. Miller about Linkern and the girls were playing like mad. We forgot everything, until finally Mitch motioned to me and we went out-doors. Mitch said: "I was goin' to have a funeral over Fanny, but I can't stand it, Skeet. Let's just you and I bury her, here by the barn." So we dug a grave and buried Fanny, and Mitch cried. And then we went into the house and went to bed.

CHAPTER VII

THE next day was Sunday, and the wonderfulest day you ever saw. We had an early breakfast, for Mr. Miller was drivin' into the country that day to preach, and Mrs. Miller was goin' with him and the girls had to get the dinner. So nobody had to go to Sunday School, and I could keep out of it by not goin' home in time. A thought came to me and I said to Mitch, "You never saw my grandpa's farm — we can walk out there before noon and have dinner, and maybe get a lift on the way. And maybe grandpa or some one will drive us in in the morning in time for school." Mitch was crazy to go and see the farm; so we struck out, down through the town, under the trestle bridge, up the hill, past Bucky Gum's big brick house, past the fair grounds and along the straight road between the wheat fields. It was wonderful, and we sang and threw clods at birds and talked over plans about goin' to see Tom Sawyer. For Mitch said: "We'll try this Old Salem place, and if that doesn't pan out, then we'll go to Hannibal. Tom'll tell us; and if he can't, we'll see his crowd anyway and have a good time. And besides, I'm lookin' forward now to somethin'. I'm goin' to lose Zueline — I feel it all through. And if I do, it's time to get away from here and forget."

"What do you mean by lose her?" says I. "You'll always be in the same town and in the same school, and you'll always be friends."

"Oh, yes," said Mitch, "but that's just the trouble —
to be in the same town and the same school and not to
have her the same. I've got a funny feelin', Skeet —
it's bound to happen. And anyway, if it don't, we must
be up and doin' and get the treasure and then square
off for somethin' else. And if I get it and all goes well,
maybe Zueline and me will marry and be happy here.
That's the way I want it."

WE SANG AND THREW CLODS

It must have been two hours before we got to the
edge of the wood where Joe Gordon lived. And I showed
Mitch the oak tree where Joe had peeled off the bark
to make tea for the rheumatism or somethin'. My
grandma had told me. Finally we crossed the bridge
over the creek, and climbed the hill. "There," I said
to Mitch, "that's my grandpa's house. Ain't it beautiful
— and look at the red barn — and over there, there's
the hills of Mason County right by Salt Creek." Mitch's
eyes fairly glowed; so then we hurried on to get to the
house, which was about half a mile.

There wasn't a soul at home but Willie Wallace, the

hired man. He was shavin' himself, goin' to see his girl,
and he let us play on his Jews harp and smell the cigars
he had in his trunk, which he had perfumed with cinnamon or somethin'. Grandpa and grandma had gone to
Concord to church, and Uncle Henry was in town seein'

GOING THROUGH THE HIRED MAN'S TRUNK

his girl, and the hired girl was off for the day. We were
hungry as wolves, so I took Mitch into the pantry where
we found a blackberry pie, and a crock of milk, rich with
cream. We ate the pie and drank the milk. Then I
showed Mitch the barn and the horses, and my saddle.
I took him into the work house where the tools were.
I showed him the telephone I made which ran down to
the tenant's house. And we got out my uncle's wagon

and played engine; and went up into the attic to look for books. Mitch found a novel by Scott and began to read; and that was the last of him. I went back to the work house and pulled a kite I had made from the rafters and got it ready to fly.

After while grandpa and grandma came from church and when grandma came out of her room where she had changed her silk dress for a calico dress in order to get dinner, I stepped out from a door and said, "Hello, grandma." "Why, child," she said, "you almost scared me to pieces. What are you doin' here? Where's your popie and your momie?" Then I told her Mitch and I had walked out, and she took me into the kitchen and made me help her. By and by she went into the pantry for somethin' and when she came out she said: "Do you like blackberry pie, Skeet?" "Yes'm," I said. "Well, I guess you do — and you like milk, too. And now you go down to the cellar and get another crock of milk — do you hear? And if I hadn't put the other pies in the cupboard in the dining room, there'd be no pie for dinner." "No, grandma, we wouldn't eat more'n one — Mitch and I wouldn't, honest we wouldn't."

Mitch came in, then, and grandma looked at him kind of close and laughed, and asked him if he was goin' to be a preacher like his pa. Well, a funny thing came out. Mr. Miller had preached at Concord that morning, and grandma began to talk about the sermon and say it was the most beautiful she ever heard. Pretty soon she went out of the room for somethin', and Mitch said: "She's the livin' image of Aunt Polly — and so she should be my grandma and not yours; for I'm Tom if anybody is, even if you're not much like Huck."

Then we had dinner, and Mitch was readin' that

novel while eatin', and grandma kept sayin', "Eat your dinner, Mitch." He did eat, but he was behind the rest of us.

We helped grandma with the dishes. Then she said, "You boys clear out while I take a rest. And after while I'll show you some things." She always took a nap after dinner, lying on a little couch under the two windows in the settin' room, where the fire-place was, and the old clock, and the mahogany chest that had come from North Carolina, given her by her grandmother, and her red-bird in a cage. Grandpa always fell asleep in his chair while reading the Petersburg *Observer*, which came the day before.

So Mitch and I walked through the orchard, and when we came back, I showed him the carriage with glass windows and the blue silk curtain; and the white horses which grandpa always drove. But we didn't put in the time very well, because we wanted grandma to wake up.

We went in the house at last, and they were talking together. I heard grandpa say something about Doc Lyon. We'd almost forgot that by now. But when we came in the room, grandma said, "Well, here you are," and went over and got out her drawer that had her trinkets in it. She had the greatest lot of pictures in rubber cases you ever saw; soldiers which were dead, and folks who had married and moved away or had died; and a watch which belonged to her son who was drowned before Mitch and I was born; and a ribbon with Linkern's picture on it; and breast pins with hair in 'em; and sticks of cinnamon. And by and by she went to her closet and got some peach leather, which Mitch had never seen before. And he thought it the best stuff he ever et. You make it by rolling peaches into a thin

leather and dryin' it, and puttin' sugar and things in it.
It's waxy like gum and chews awful well.

Then she got down her scrap book and read little things
that Ben Franklin said, about temperance and work,
and study, and savin' money. She asked Mitch if he
had read the Bible through, and Mitch said yes, for he
had. "You haven't," she said to me — "if you'll read

GRANDMA SHOWING HER TREASURES

it through, I'll give you five dollars." So I promised.
"Now," she said, "you can do it by fall if you're industrious. Work and play — play hard and work hard, for
the night cometh when no man can work." I never
saw Mitch happier than he was this afternoon. The
time slipped by, and finally grandma said to me to bring
in the cows, she was goin' to milk. We began to wonder how we'd get back to town. But we went for the
cows just the same and watched grandma milk, and
helped her with the buckets, and watched her feed her

F

cats. Then we said we must go, at least after supper. "How can you go?" said grandma, "you can't walk to-night. It's too far. Willie Wallace is going in town early with a load of corn, and you can ride." That suited us. So we had supper, fried mush and eggs and milk. Then we had prayers; and grandma put us in the west room up-stairs where there was a picture of Alfaratta, the Indian maid. And I think we would be sleepin' yet if she hadn't come in to wake us.

We rode in with Willie Wallace and got to the school yard before eight o'clock. Mitch and I agreed that this was the longest school day we ever spent.

CHAPTER VIII

SCHOOL interfered a good deal with huntin' treasure, but things happened now and then to let us out. The professor looked exactly like Tom Sawyer's teacher, except ours wore a beard. He seemed awful old and kind of knotty and twisty. I think he must have been near sixty, and he had been a preacher, and lost his pulpit and so turned to teachin'. We could see he was pretty rusty about a lot of things. You can't fool boys much, and you couldn't fool Mitch and me.

The professor's name was Professor Taylor. He had a low forehead with his hair lyin' flat like a wig

PROFESSOR TAYLOR

— and creases across his forehead where he had been worryin'. And one of his shoulders was kind of humped up and to one side, and one of his hands had a stiff thumb. He couldn't keep order in the school at all, because some of the big boys like Charley King and George Heigold kept somethin' goin' all the time. And these big boys got the rest of us into things like throwin' chalk and sometimes erasers, or all together droppin' our geographies of a sudden. Then the professor would tap the bell and say, "The tap of the bell is the voice of the teacher — who dropped their geographies, who was it?" Then things would get worse and there would be a noise like a political meetin'. Pa said he warn't fit to run a school, but the directors kept him in because he was related to the president of the board. And most every mornin' for exercises he would read the 19th psalm, which says, "The law of the Lord is perfect, converting the soul; the testimony of the Lord is sure, making wise the simple," generally lookin' at me when he said " simple," because I couldn't learn very well. Then he would start the song with a tuning fork, "Too-do" and generally somebody would cough like he had a awful cold and so start the noise. Then lots would cough and he'd have to wait before singin' "The Shades of Night Was Falling Fast." Then he would talk to us about bein' good. And onct when Ella Stephens died over at Springfield, where she had been for some kind of a operation, you couldn't find out what, because nobody would say, he got up and said that God would forgive Ella and all of us should pray for her. Most of us cried, rememberin' Ella's red cheeks and how she used to laugh when she came in the schoolroom. She was about 16.

And one mornin' school seemed to go all to pieces. This George Heigold was studyin' geometry and he came to me and says, before school took up: "When I go to the blackboard to demonstrate in geometry, I'll wink at you and then you drop your reader or somethin', Mitch will do the same, and then I'll get through, I'll show you. For I ain't studied the lesson." I said " all right."

So when the geometry class was recitin', there was four in it, George and Charley King, and Bertha Whitney and Mary Pitkin, the girls bein' awful smart, and always havin' their lessons. The professor turned to George Heigold and says : " George, you may demonstrate proposition three." Then the professor gave Bertha proposition four, and Mary proposition five, and Charley proposition six. But meantime George didn't get up to draw his figure on the blackboard, though the rest did. He was lookin' in the book so he could draw it; and finally the professor said, "Did you hear me, George?" "Yes, sir," said George, "but I was tryin' to think out a different way to demonstrate this here proposition from the way the book says." And the professor says : "If you demonstrate it the way the book does, that will be very well, and I'll give you a hundred." So then George hopped right up and drew a fine figure on the board and lettered it, and was just about to set down and study the book, as I could see, because he was eyein' the professor and expectin' that some of the others would be called on first, and while the professor was watchin' somebody else demonstrate, he would study up. But it happened wrong : George was called on first. So he got up, lookin' at me to give me the wink, and he began : "Supposin' A-B is a straight line, and supposin' B-C is a straight line, and supposin' C-D is a straight line, and supposin' these here lines are all joined so as to make a triangle." Then the professor got to his side and made it so George couldn't see me to wink, and he says : "No, no, George." And George says, "Very well, I have a original demonstration." And the professor says : "Original, original — just follow the book, just follow the book." Of course, George couldn't, and so he stepped back and gave me the wink, and I dropped my reader, Mitch dropped his reader. Percy Guyer, an awful nervous boy, started like, and flung his ink well off. Then there was a lot of coughin' and some laughin', and the professor went wild and says, "What is the matter? What can be the matter now?" And he turned to George and says, in a mad way, "Take your seat." So George did, and began to study the demonstration. And after while it got quiet and the professor went on with Mary and Bertha who got a hundred. Charley King got through fair, and probably got 75. And there sat George and the class was about to be dismissed without George recitin', when George raised his hand and said : "I'll do my best to demonstrate the way you want me to. I don't want to lose my chance." So the professor just smiled awful friendly on George and says " all right." And George got up and recited perfect, according to the book and got 100. I never saw such a boy as George Heigold ; for once the professor got up an astronomy class — the whole school mostly was in it — and he was teachin' us general things about the stars and what they was made of. So one day the professor called out quick as a test of what he had told us before : "What element is found on the planet Mars that is not found anywhere else in the universe?" And George Heigold who was sittin' way back yelled out "Sapolio" — and the whole school went wild, into a roar of laugh. While the professor marched up and down flippin' his coat tails with his hands and sayin', "Who said Sapolio? Who said Sapolio?" But no one told and he couldn't find out.

So on this day when George Heigold got a hundred in geometry, somethin' else happened. It was a warm

day and you could hear bees outside, and the trees was
beginnin' to show green. All of us was so sleepy we
could hardly stay awake, and I could look out of the
window and see the river and the hills on the other side,
and I could even see people fishin'. Well, near noon we
all began to smell somethin' like onions, and it got worse
and worse, and seemed to come up from the registers,
for Jas. Walker, the janitor, was keepin' a little fire yet,
or had for early mornin'. And the professor got over
the register and smelt and he
says, "Who put asoefetida in
the furnace — who did such a
cowherd thing as that?" Nobody said nothin'. It was a
surprise to me, and to Mitch,
but we were tickled for we
could see what was comin'.
The smell got worse and worse,
and Jas. Walker came runnin'
through the room and lookin'
in registers. Then everybody

LOOKING FOR ASAFETIDA

began to cough in earnest, only George Heigold coughed
louder than a cow, and Bertha Whitney, bein' delicate,
fainted and there was a lot of runnin' to her, pickin' her
up and fetchin' her water. And the schoolroom went
wild. The professor lost hold of everything and got white
and walked back and forth flappin' his coat tails with
his hands. Till finally he said, "School's dismissed for
the day." Then we all got up and busted out, singing
and laughing. So Mitch and me went to dinner and then
hurried off to Old Salem to dig for treasure.

When we got to the mill, Jim Lally was already there
and was fishin' and had caught a big cat. They was

bitin' good. And he says : "How did you boys like the asoefetida?" We said "pretty well." And then he said, "If anybody says I did that and you tell it, I'll lick you both, so you can't stand up." Jim was 16 or 17 and big and we knew he meant it. But Mitch laughed and said : "Why would we tell it? Ain't we off for the afternoon the same as you?"

So we went up and dug, but didn't find nothin'. And finally while we was diggin' away, all of a sudden I saw a big snake in the weeds, all coiled, and Mitch didn't see it at first. For all of a sudden it kind of sprang out like a spring you let loose and bit Mitch on the hand. Mitch gave an awful cry and began to suck the place where the snake bit him. I says, "Don't do that, Mitch, you have a tooth out, and the pisen will get in you there. What's the use of takin' it out one place and puttin' it in another?" I grabbed a stick then and killed the snake. Mitch got pale and began to be sickish and I was scared to death. And we ran down to the road as fast as we could. Just then a wagon came along, and I hollered to the man; so he came over and lifted Mitch into the wagon and laid him down, and we put the snake into the wagon too, for I had carried it along; and the man whipped up his horses fast so as to get into town for a doctor.

Mitch's hand didn't swell, but he kept gettin' sicker and sicker, and was moanin' and about to die; and the man drove faster and faster, for he said the snake was one of the most pisen. When we got to the square, Mr. Miller happened to be walkin' along. And the man drew up and said to Mr. Miller, "Here's your boy, bit by a snake." "What kind?" says Mr. Miller, all excited. "Here he is," said the man, and held up the snake. Mr. Miller says: "Oh, fiddlesticks! That's a blue racer, as harmless as the peck of a chicken." Then he took hold of Mitch and shook him and says: "Here, Mitch, this is all foolishness — you're just scart; that snake ain't pisen. He can't hurt you more than a chicken." So Mitch sat right up and looked at his hand which wasn't swelled. And he says: "I am pisened, I'm sick." "Oh, shucks," said Mr. Miller. "It's just imagination. Come into the drug store and get a soda."

Mitch climbed out of the wagon, kind of pale yet, but more sheepish and went in and drank his soda and began to laugh. And Mr. Miller said, "Where was you?" And Mitch said, "Down by the mill." And Mr. Miller said, "Now, listen; you've had a scare, but there is only two snakes around here that is pisen. One is the copperhead. You can tell him by his bright copper-colored head and his strawberry body; the other is the rattlesnake. You can tell him by his rattle. But if you don't be careful foolin' around in the woods and dreamin' and not watchin' what you're doin', one of them will bite you. Now look here, you go home and get in the wood and help around the house." So Mitch says, "Come on, Skeet, and help me, and for company." So I went and helped Mitch with his work.

CHAPTER IX

AFTER that Saturday that we made garden, we tried our best to get out to Old Salem on Saturdays, but something always happened, except one Saturday. One time I had to make garden again, one time I had to help Mitch make garden, another time pa and ma went to Pleasant Plains to a picnic and I had to stay and take care of Little Billie, for Myrtle went, because I had gone with pa and ma somewhere, I forget where it was, and it was Myrtle's time. Somehow Myrtle was always in my way, but ma said I was selfish and I suppose I was. Finally on the Saturday before school let out, we went to Old Salem, taking two shovels and two picks. We didn't do much, just looked around, and found a lot of foundations where buildings had been when the village was there, and got the lay of the land. We left our tools with the miller at the mill. He said all right, but told us to wait for the next rainbow, and then follow it up and get a bag of gold. "Never you mind," said Mitch. "Others have found treasure and so can we." He told the miller we were digging in the woods, because he said to me if it leaks out we're after these old cellars and places, there'll be a slough of diggers out here lookin' for treasure, and they'll get it before we do.

But first after school was out something interfered with our goin' on. It was this: Robbins' Circus had come to town, and his son, who was awful handsome, was a bareback rider, and had set the town wild, and Zueline came to Mitch and made him get up a circus. That took time, for we had to practice.

We went to the real circus, Mitch and me, and earned the money ourselves. It was this way: Pa said, "You boys spend so much time foolin' around about treasures, why don't you earn some money?" So Mitch's pa made up a lot of pop-corn balls and we sold 'em on the street and got money that way to see the show. It was the most beautiful circus in the world — such lovely ladies, and a clown who sang "Never Take the Horseshoe from the Door."

Then we got to work to get up our circus. Zueline had her Ayrdale and we cooped him up for a lion; we put the cat in a box for a tiger, and the rooster for an ostrich, and Mitch caught a snake, and I had my pony to play Robbins' son, and Myrtle was goin' to be the woman who et fire. Mitch practiced for the trapeze, and he had to practice a lot, for when he was 4 or 5 years old, he cut his foot in two with an ax, and after that the toes were a little numb and didn't work as well as they did before.

Mitch said that in Europe they had a royal box for queens and princesses, so he built a kind of box for Zueline to sit in, and see the circus, and draped it with rag carpets and put a mirror in it. It was awful pretty.

Mitch was gate-keeper and manager. We had some bills printed by Onstott, the printer, which said "Miller & Kirby's Renowned Circus and Menagerie" and a lot of things, naming the performers and all that. But I must say we had our troubles. First Kit O'Brien and his gang came down to break up the show. He tried to come in without payin', but Mitch settled old scores this time. He hit Kit a punch in the mouth and knocked out his baby teeth, which were danglin' and needed to be pulled anyway. He bled like a pig and ran up the hill hollerin', "I'll get even." But that settled that.

Then Myrtle burned her mouth trying to chew cotton on fire, and Mitch's toe went back on him while hangin' from the trapeze. He fell, but didn't hurt himself much; only the audience laughed, even the princess Zueline in the box. I rode the pony pretty well, but he was too big for the ring in the barn, and Charley King who tried to sing "Never Take the Horseshoe from the Door" forgot part of it, and had to back into the corn crib which was the dressin' room.

Outside of these things, the show was a success — only this was the day Mitch began to get acquainted with Charley King and George Heigold, which was a bad thing, as I'll tell later.

So the circus was over and we took up the treasure again. Mitch said — we mustn't let another thing interfere. And so we went to work at Old Salem.

As I said, we found a lot of old foundations and we scraped and dug around in all of 'em, mostly; and I never see so many snakes. Mitch could take a snake by the tail and crack his head off like a whip; but I was afraid to see him do it because there was hoop snakes around, and their tails is pisen. Nigger Dick told me he saw one roll down hill one time and just as it got to an oak tree, it took its tail out of its mouth and struck the tree with the stinger of its tail. The next morning all the leaves on the tree was withered. That is how pisen a hoop snake is. Well, of course there was lots of black snakes and they can wrap you. One wrapped

Kit O'Brien once; and he waited till it got itself so tight that you could see through its skin, then he touched it with a knife and it bust in two and fell off of him.

Well, we didn't find a thing, though once when we struck some tin cans, I thought sure we'd hit it.

By and by one day when we was diggin', I looked up and saw an old feller standin' watchin' us. He was awful old, maybe more than eighty, and he just looked at Mitch and me and finally said, "Lost somethin', boys?" Mitch said: "I suppose you might say so till we find it." Then the old feller said: "I hope you'll find it, for you look hot workin' here in this hot sun, and you are workin', I declare." Mitch's face was red and he looked earnest, and I suppose I did too.

I don't know whether the old feller had talked to the miller or what, but finally he said, " 'Tain't likely you'll find any treasure here. It's all been taken away long ago. Every place is like a mine, it produces a certain amount and that's all. This place produced great riches, boys, but it's a worked out place now. It's a dead mine." Then he stopped a minute and talked to himself a little and looked around and said: "Yep, this is the founda- tion of the Rutledge Tavern where Linkern lived. Yep, I know because right over there is where Dr. Allen lived; and over this a way was preacher Cameron's house, and here was the road, and down yonder was Linkern and Berry's store, and back thar was Offets store. Yep, it all comes back to me now. There was more'n twenty houses here, shops, stores, schoolhouses, and this tavern; and here Linkern lived, and I've seen him many a time around here. And I'm glad to see you boys diggin' here for you might find treasure. Peter Lukins, the shoe- maker had his place just three houses over, right there, and he was a miser, and they thought he hid his money sommers around here."

"Well," said Mitch, under his breath, "no more cheating to the county. Law or no law, if we find it there, your pa will never know it. We've had one experience and that's enough." So he said out loud to the old feller — "Where is Peter Lukins' place?" And the old feller said : "Climb out of thar and I'll show you."

We walked over about a hundred yards maybe, and here was another foundation all full of dead weeds and new weeds, and so grown up you could hardly see the stones at first, and not a stick of timber left, except a log lying outside the foundation. The older feller sat down and began to talk.

"I left this country in '65," he said, "for California, and now I'm back to Menard County, Illinois, to die and be buried with my people over at Rock Creek. And I'm goin' about seein' the old places onct again. You see, there ain't anything left of the village of Salem, but it all comes back to me, and I can close my eyes and see the people that used to walk around here, and see Linkern. And I'll tell you a story of a man who found treasure here."

Mitch looked awful eager and bright-eyed, and the old feller twisted off some tobacco and began to chew and get the thread of his story.

"It was this a way," he began. "There was a man here who was clerkin' in one of the stores ; and one day a feller drove up and said 'hallow' and this clerk came out of the store and says, 'What is it?' The traveler says, 'Here's a barl I have no use for and don't want to carry on my wagon any furder, and I'll sell it to you.' And the clerk says, 'I ain't got no use for the barl.' 'Well,' says the traveler, 'you can have it for fifty cents, and it will accommodate me; and besides I don't want to just throw it away.' So the clerk says all right, and gave him fifty cents and took the barl in the store and put it in the corner. It was kind of heavy too — had somethin' in it — had treasure in it, as you'll see. And after a few days this here clerk took the barl and turned it upside down and there was treasure."

"How much?" said Mitch. "Gee, but that was wonderful."

"Well," said the old feller, "you can believe it or not, it was treasure too much to count. You've heard of a man bein' suddenly rich and not realizin' it, or havin' somethin' given to him that he didn't know the value of, and findin' out afterwards. It was just this way."

"Well," said Mitch, "why didn't he count it, right away, or was it diamonds or rubies?"

"He couldn't count it all right there. It couldn't be done, because it had to be weighed and tested and tried out, and put on the market; for you might say some of it was rubies, and to know what rubies are worth takes experience and time and a lot of things."

Mitch got more and more interested and I did too. Then the old feller went on.

"But that ain't sayin' that this clerk didn't know it was treasure — he did — but it was treasure that he had to put work on to bring out all its value."

"Melt it up," said Mitch, "or polish it maybe."

"Yes," said the old feller, "melt it up and polish it, and put his elbow grease on it. And nobody but him could do it. He couldn't hire it done. For if he had, he'd a lost the treasure—the cost of doin' that would have wasted all the treasure. And this the clerk knew.

That's why he didn't know what it was worth, though he
knew it was worth a lot and he was a happy man."

"Well," said Mitch, "what was it — tell me — I
can't wait."

"Books," said the old feller — "two law books.
Blackstone's Commentaries."

"Oh, shucks," said Mitch.

"Shucks," said the old man. "Listen to me. Here
you boys dig in the sun like niggers for treasure, and you'll
never find it that a way. It ain't to be found. And if
you did, it wouldn't amount to nothin'. But suppose
you get a couple of books into your head like Abe Linkern
did, and become a great lawyer, and a president, and a
benefactor to your fellows, then you have found treasure
and given it too. And it was out of that barl that Linkern became what he was. He found his treasure there.
He might have found it sommers else; but at least he
found it there. And you can't get treasure that's good
that the good of you wasn't put into it in getting it.
Remember that. If you dug up treasure here, what
have you put into the getting of that treasure? Just
your work with the shovel and the pick — that's all —
and you haven't got rich doin' that. The money will
go and you'll be where you was before. But if there's
good in you, and you put the good into what you find
and make it all it can be made, then you have found
real treasure like Linkern did."

Mitch was quiet for a minute and then said: "Don't
you 'spose the man who sold the barl to Linkern knew
the books was in there? Of course he did. And if he
did, why didn't he take the books and study and be president? He couldn't, that's why. If you call books treasure, they ain't unless they mean something to you. But

take money or jewels, who is there that they don't mean
somethin' to? Nobody. Why there're hundreds of
books around our house, that would do things if they
meant anything. And I've found my book. It's 'Tom
Sawyer.' And till I find another I mean to stick by it, as
fur as that goes. One book at a time."

I don't know where Mitch got all this talk. He was
the wonderfulest boy that ever lived, but besides he heard
his pa talk things all the time, and his pa could talk Greek
and knew everything in the world.

We sat talkin' to this old feller till pretty near sundown,
when we said we must go. We threw the tools into
Peter Lukins' cellar and started off, leavin' the old feller
standin'. When we got to the edge of the hill which led
down to the road by the river, we turned around and
looked, and saw the old feller standin' there still, black
like against the light of the sun. Mitch was awful
serious.

"It must be awful to be old like that," said Mitch.
"Did you hear what he said — come back to Menard
County to be buried with his folks — and all his folks
gone. How does a feller live when he comes to that?
Nothin' to do, nowhere really to go. Skeeters, sometimes I wisht I was dead. Even this treasure business,
as much fun as it is, is just a never endin' trouble and
worry. And I see everybody in the same fix, no matter
who they are, worryin' about somethin'. And while it
seems I've lived for ever and ever, and it looks thousands
of miles back to the time I cut my foot off, just the same,
I seem to be close to the beginnin' too, and sometimes
I can just feel myself mixin' into the earth and bein'
nothin'."

"Don't you believe in heaven, Mitch?" says I.

G

"No," he says, "not very clear."

"And you a preacher's son!"

"That's just it," says Mitch. "A preacher's son is like a circus man's son, young Robbins who was here. There's no mystery about it. Why, young Robbins paid no attention to the horses, animals, the band — things we went crazy about. And I see my father get ready for funerals and dig up his old sermons for funerals and all that, till it looks just like any trade to me. But besides, how can heaven be, and what's the use? No, sir, I don't want to be buried with my folks — I want to be lost, like your uncle was, and buried by the Indians way off where nobody knows."

Then Mitch switched and began to talk about Tom Sawyer again. He said we're the age of Tom Sawyer; that Linkern was a grown man when he found the books; that there was a time for everything, that as far as that's concerned, Tom might be working on something else now, having found his treasure. "Why, lookee, don't the book end up with Tom organizing a robbers' gang to rob the rich — not harm anybody, mind you — but really do good — take money away from them that got it wrong and don't need it, and give it to the poor that can't get it and do need it?"

By this time we was clost to town. The road ran under a hill where there was the old grave-yard, where lots of soldiers was buried. "Do you know," said Mitch, "them pictures your grandma had of soldiers stay in my mind. They looked old and grown up with beards and everything; but after all, they're not so old — and they went away and was killed and lots of 'em are buried up there — some without names. Think of it, Skeet. Suppose there should be a war again and you'd go, and be blown up so no one could know you, and they'd put you in a grave with no stone."

"Ain't that what you want, Mitch?"

"Yes, but you're different, Skeet. And besides, it's different dyin' natural and bein' buried by the Indians in a lovely place, and bein' killed like an animal and dumped with a lot of others and no stone. If every boy felt as I do, they'd never be another war. They couldn't get me into a war except to defend the country, and it would have to be a real defense. You know, Skeet, we came here from Missouri, where there was awful times during the war; and my pa thinks the war could have been avoided. He used to blame Linkern, but he don't no more. Say, did you think of Linkern while we were diggin' to-day? I did. I could feel him. The sky spoke about him, the still air spoke about him, the meadow larks reminded me of him. Onct I thought I saw him."

"No, Mitch."

"Yes, sir — you see I see things, Skeet, sometimes spirits, and I hear music most of the time, and the fact is, nobody knows me."

"Nor me," says I. "I'm a good deal lonelier than you are, Mitch Miller, and nobody understands me either; and I have no girl. Girls seem to me just like anything else — dogs or chickens — I don't mean no disrespect — but you know."

By this time we'd got to Petersburg, and up to a certain corner, and we'd been talking about Linkern so much that a lot of things came to me. And I says: "See this corner, Mitch? I'll tell you somethin' about it — maybe to-morrow."

CHAPTER X

THE next day as I was helpin' Myrtle bury her doll, Mitch came by and whistled. I had made a coffin out of a cigar box, and put glass in for a window to look through at the doll's face, and we had just got the grave filled. I went out to the front gate and there was Charley King and George Heigold with Mitch. They were big boys about fourteen and knew a lot of things we didn't. They hunted with real guns and roasted chickens they hooked over in Fillmore's woods. They carried slings and knucks and used to go around with grown men, sometimes Joe Pink. I didn't like to have Mitch friends with these boys. It hurt me; and I was afraid of something, and they were not very friendly to me for some reason. But a few times I went to Charley King's to stay all night. His mother was a strange woman. She petted Charley like the mother did in the " Fourth Reader " whose boy was hanged because he had no raisin' and was given his own way about everything. Mrs. King used to look at me and say I had pretty eyes and take me on her lap and stroke my head. She was a queer woman, and Charley's father was off somewhere, Chandlerville, or somewhere, and they said they didn't live together. My ma stopped me goin' to Mrs. King's, and so as Charley ran with George Heigold, that's probably why I didn't like Mitch to be with them, as I wasn't very friendly any more with Charley on account of this.

These two boys went off somewhere and left us when we got to the square. And then I took Mitch to see something.

The tables was now turned. I did most of the talkin' — though Mitch was more interestin' than me, and that's why he says more than I do in this book. We went to that corner where we was the day before, and I says to Mitch: "Look at this house partly in the street, and look at the street how it jogs. Well, Linkern did that. You see he surveyed this whole town of Petersburg. But as to this, this is how it happened. You see it was after the Black Hawk War in 1836, and when Linkern came here to survey, he found that Jemima Elmore, which was a widow of Linkern's friend in the war, had a piece of land, and had built a house on it and was livin' here with her children. And Linkern saw if the street run straight north and south, a part of her house would be in the street. So to save Jemima's house, he set his compass to make the line run a little furder south. And so this is how the line got skewed and leaves this strip kind of irregular, clear through the town, north and south. This is what I call makin' a mistake that is all right, bein' good and bad at the same time."

And Mitch says: "A man that will do that is my kind. And yet pa used to say that freein' the slaves was not the thing; and maybe Linkern skewed the line there and left a strip clear across the country that will always be irregular and bad."

"Anyway," said Mitch, "do you know what I think? I think there ain't two boys in the world that live in as good a town as this. What's Tom Sawyer's town? Nothin' without Tom Sawyer — no great men but Tom Sawyer, and he ain't a man yet. There ain't anybody in his book that can't be matched by some one in this town — but there's no one in his book to equal Linkern, and this is Linkern's town.　And I've been thinkin' about it."

I says : "There you have it, Mitch.　It's true.　We're the luckiest boys in the world to live here where Linkern lived, and to hear about him from people who knew him, to see this here house where he made a mistake, though doin' his best, to hear about them books, and to walk over the ground where he lived at Salem, and more than that, to have all this as familiar to us as Nigger Dick or Joe Pink."

"It's too familiar," said Mitch.　"My pa says we won't appreciate it or understand it all for years to come."

So I went on tellin' Mitch how my grandpa hired Linkern once in a lawsuit; then we went to the court house, for I wanted to show Mitch some things I knew about.

The court house was a square brick building with a hall running through it, and my pa's office, the coroner's office, the treasurer's office on each side of the hall.　And there was a big yard around the court house, with watermelon rinds scattered over the grass; and a fence around the yard and a hitch rack where the farmers tied their teams. And at one side there was a separate building where the clerks of the courts had their offices.　I knew all the lay of the land.　So I took Mitch into the clerk's office and showed him papers which Linkern had written and signed. At first he wouldn't believe it.　So while we was lookin' at them papers, John Armstrong came in to pay his taxes or somethin' and he knew me because him and my pa had played together as boys.　He was a brother of Duff which Linkern had defended for murder, and I tried to get him to tell Mitch and me about the trial, but he didn't have time, and he said : "The next time you come to your grandpap's, come over to see me. I live about 7 miles from your grandpap. And I'll tell you and play the fiddle for you."

"When can we come?" says Mitch.

"Any time," says John.

"To-morrow," says Mitch.

"Wal, to-morrow I'm goin' to Havaner — But you just get your grandpap to drive you and Mitch over some day, and we'll have a grand visit." So he went away.

Then as we was comin' out of the clerk's office, Sheriff Rutledge stepped up and read a subpoena to Mitch and me to appear before the Grand Jury in August, about Doc Lyon.

"We won't be here," says Mitch.

"Why not?" says the sheriff. "Where'll you be?"

This stumped Mitch — he didn't want to say. The sheriff walked away and Mitch says : "Now I see what we have to do. We must clean up that Peter Lukins' cellar right off and get off to Hannibal to see Tom. One thing will happen after another if we let it, and we'll never get away, and never see Tom. I wish this here Doc Lyon was in Halifax."

Says I, "Who wanted to talk to him in the jail, you or me?"

"Why, I did," said Mitch.

"Well, then, you made the tangle, Mitch, and we'll have to stick. For it's a jail offense to run away from a subpoena, my pa says so, and we are witnesses, and will have to stick."

"Well, then," says Mitch, "if we do, and the whole month of August goes by, and school commences before we get off, we'll throw the school and go anyway. My mind is made up. Dern it, I never dreamed of gettin' tangled in the law for a little thing like seein' Doc Lyon in jail. It's awful. Look here, you go to your pa and get me off and get off yourself."

I knew I couldn't do that, that pa wouldn't do it, and I said so. And Mitch looked terribly worried. And he said, "Let's go out to Salem and finish up Peter Lukins' — right now."

The air seemed to sing with the heat, and it was awful hot down in that place among the weeds. We worked like beavers getting the weeds away so we could pick into the stones and the dirt. My, it was hard work. And we hadn't been there more'n an hour when I heard some one cryin' and hollerin'. We looked over the edge of the cellar and here came Heine Missman's brother, wringin' his hands and cryin', and actin' like he was crazy. "Heine's drowned," he cried, "Heine's drowned."

We climbed out of the cellar as quick as we could and ran down to the mill, for John, Heine's brother, said that Heine had stepped into the mill race.

"Is the mill runnin'?" said Mitch.

"No," said John.

"Because if it is," said Mitch, "he's all ground up by now in the wheels."

But the mill hadn't run that day, so if we could get Heine out, we could save him maybe. John couldn't swim, nor Heine. And John said that Heine had stepped into the race, thinkin' he could wade over to the dam, and he went down and down, and then didn't come up any more. John had tried to catch him by the hair, but couldn't.

We were good divers, both Mitch and me, and finally I dived and got a hold of his shirt and brought him up. But he was all swelled, and blue in the face, and was dead. He'd been in about an hour before we got him.

Just then the miller came up and saw what had happened. He went and got his wagon and put Heine's body in it, and we all drove into town; and finally to

I BROUGHT HEINE UP

Heine's house, where his mother fainted and cried so you could hear her all over town.

Then Mitch and me started for home. Mitch was awful solemn and said, "That might have been you or me, Skeet. What does it mean, anyway? Here's Heine just growin' up, just been around this town with us boys a few years, and now he's drowned and gone for good. Why, I can remember when he wore short dresses, and now it's all over, and it looks like life is just nuthin'."

Then, after a bit, he said, "I have a presentiment."

"What's that?" I asked.

"Why, it's when you know somethin' is goin' to hap-pen."

"Do you mean somethin' 's goin' to happen, to you or me, Mitch?"

"Well, nothin' like drownin' or dyin'," said Mitch. "I don't get it that way. But I just feel we'll never dig any more at Old Salem."

"But we ain't finished there," says I.

"That may be," he says, "but to-morrow is Sunday, and I've always noticed that the next week after Sunday ain't the same."

We got to my gate now, and Mitch hardly said " good-by " — just went on lookin' down at the ground. I watched him till he got up the hill and up to Tom White's, then I turned in.

CHAPTER XI

SUNDAY School bothered me terribly, for a lot of reasons. I had to dress up, for one thing, and in the summer time ma made me wear linen suits, which was starched stiff by Delia, our girl. They had sharp edges which scratched. And my hat was too small, and my shoes hurt. And the inside of the church smelt like stale coffee grounds, and the teacher looked hungry and kept parting her lips with a sound as if she was gettin' ready to eat, or wanted to, and she trickled inside like the sound of water or somethin'. Besides, there was no end to the Bible stories and the golden texts.

Mitch and the Miller girls went just as if it was the thing to do, and they didn't seem to mind it. It was a part of their life. But it was a little different with Mitch after all, for sometimes he didn't go. He went mostly, but he stayed away if he wanted to read, and his pa let him alone. Mr. Miller was the best man you ever saw, and everybody loved him.

It was this way with us children, ma made us go and pa said nothin' about it unless she asked him to make us go, and then he'd say "go on now." But he didn't go himself, or much to church either. I never understood him, he was kind of a mystery.

Well, on a Sunday in July me and Myrtle was dressed to go and waitin' for ma to dress Little Billie. It was awful hot and looked like rain, and my clothes scratched,

my shoes hurt; but Myrtle was all quiet and anxious to
go. Little Billie was frettin', like he allus did. He
didn't want to go; and ma was just buttonin' his dress,
and had the bowl near to comb his hair out of. And he
kept frettin' and sayin' he didn't want to go. By and
by ma shook him and said: "You never want to go. I
never see such heathen children. None of you want to
go." "I do," says Myrtle. "Yes," says ma, "you do.

SUNDAY SCHOOL

You're good. But Billie and Skeet make this same
trouble every Sunday." Then Little Billie began to
cry worse, and said his throat hurt him, and ma said,
"Let me see." So she looked, and his throat had white
splotches, and she said, "Land of the livin'," and began
to undress him. His head was hot, too. So she put
Myrtle and me out of the room and told us to go and
play, and we needn't go to Sunday School. I changed
back to my old clothes and went out under the oak tree.

Pretty soon the doctor came — Doctor Holland. He drank a lot, but was the smartest doctor in town, just the same. And he and pa quarreled sometimes, but they were friends; for pa said Doc Holland meant no harm, even when he threatened to kill, which he did lots of times, even my pa. It turned out that Little Billie had the diphtheria and the next day he was as sick as a child could be, and live. They did everything for him, even got a kind of a lamp to blow carbolic acid in his throat; but he got no better. And I never saw my pa so worked up; it showed us what child he loved the most. He was about frantic and so was ma, and neither of 'em slept at all, it seemed.

Of course while Little Billie was sick, we dropped the diggin' out at Salem — I was helpin' around the house. And Mitch said he had no heart for it. He came onct to see Little Billie and just looked at him and began to cry and went away. Little Billie was unconscious and didn't know Mitch.

And grandma came in and helped. She wanted to give Little Billie some tea she could make from some weeds she'd heard about — but the doctor said it wouldn't do any good. So she just helped and let ma and the doctor run it; and the house just smelt of carbolic acid from that spray-lamp, and Little Billie gettin' worse every day. Grandpa came in onct, and went in and looked at him, and took his hand, and then just walked out of the room, and stood out in the yard a bit, and bent down and picked some leaves and began to pull 'em apart. I went out and said: "Is he better, grandpa?" But he didn't answer for quite a spell. Then he said — "The little feller's gone" and walked away.

So one night when he'd been sick about two weeks, it

was about eight o'clock, and all of a sudden Little Billie's eyes opened big. There had been a lot of runnin' around that day; pa was cryin' and the doctor was there all day. As I said, Little Billie opened his eyes big, and ma was settin' right by the bed and pa was standin' there, and Myrtle and me was standin' at the door lookin' in, for they wouldn't let us in the room. Then all of a sudden Little Billie said, "Sing somethin', ma," and she began to sing "Flee as a Bird to its Mountain," without her voice breakin' or anything; but she'd only sang a little when she broke into a great cry and pa cried, for Little Billie had died — just in a second, it seemed. So Myrtle and me ran out-doors and began to cry, and I got down in the grass and rolled and cried.

So I was lyin' there, lookin' up at the stars, quiet for a bit, and pretty soon my pa called me, and said, "Come on with me." So we started down town together to get the undertaker. And just as we got to Harris' barn, there were clouds way up that looked like gates with the moon shining between 'em, and I said to pa, "Is that where Little Billie went through into heaven?" "Yep," said pa, just cold like, hard and cold as if there warn't a thing to it, and he was half mad at me for askin' such a question; then he went on: "Some day you'll understand — but life is just a trouble and tangle. I've been messed up all my life; always getting ready to do something, never really getting anything done. The Civil War has made a lot of trouble — trouble and enemies for me, because I didn't believe in it. And I've had to fight my way through, and work like a slave and worry about money matters, and I've never found my treasure any more than you boys have, or if I ever did, something took it away, like you lost Nancy Allen's money. And now

Little Billie is dead, and I don't care what happens next."

Pa scared me with his talk; and when we got to the undertaker's, he rattled the door, and old Moore came out, and pa said, "My little boy's dead, come up," in a tired voice, or kind of hard, or somethin'.

Then there was the funeral. All the Miller children came and Zueline and her mother, and lots of grown men who knew my father or loved Little Billie for his own sake; and grandpa and grandma and Uncle Henry, and John Armstrong drove clear in from his farm — only Mitch didn't come. And I wasn't there, either, for now I had the diphtheria, too. Only they told me about it; how Mr. Miller spoke so beautiful, how the tears streamed down his face, as he talked, and how all the children cried. And this was two days after Little Billie died, and I was out of my head and havin' awful dreams.

At first when I took sick, I expected to die, of course, and I thought about all my life, until I got cloudy and began to fly and talk wild. I thought about all I was goin' to miss, never to see Mitch again, not to see any more Christmases; but somehow, I didn't regret anything much I had done and wasn't exactly afraid. I wasn't sorry about not likin' Sunday School or anything — only it just seemed that I had never done anything, or learned anything. We hadn't found the treasure — I had never had a real friend but Mitch; I never loved a girl. I just seemed to myself a shadow that had moved around seein' things, but not being seen, and always alone and lonely, havin' my best times flyin' kites or when I wasn't with Mitch. I didn't seem real to myself, and it got worse and worse, until I got delirious and became a dozen boys, doin' every sort of thing. And first thing

I knew, my ma was feedin' me out of a spoon.   I was so
weak I couldn't lift a hand.   But I had come to and was
on the mend.   It all seemed strange to wake up and find
Little Billie gone and remember back.   Ma looked worn
out and wouldn't answer questions about Mitch or anything.   I had been sick more'n two weeks, and all but
died.   By and by I began to mend, and then I could sit
up, and one day Mitch came to see me.   It was the first
day I was dressed, and had begun to walk a little.

CHAPTER XII

MA brought Mitch in the room, and said : "Have a good visit now, for we're goin' to send Skeet to the farm. He needs it, and I'm worn out. Your grandpa is comin' on Saturday, and they want you out there for a while, and it will do you good."

Mitch looked a minute and said : "I'll miss you, but there's nothing to do here." Then when ma went out of the room, he said : "The jig's up at Salem. I dug the Peter Lukins' cellar out, and there's nothing there, and nothing at Salem. So it's us for Tom Sawyer." Then he fished some letters out of his pocket and handed one to me to read. "This is your writin', Mitch," I said. "I know it," says Mitch — "But wait, read this, and I'll show you somethin'." This is what it said :

" Dear Tom : My name is Mitch Miller, and I live here in Petersburg, as you'll see. My chum is Skeet Kirby, a boy as good as Huckleberry Finn, but different, as you'll see when you meet him. But you'll like him. He's sick now, but he's true blue, and when he gets up, we want to come to see you. For we've dug for treasure all around here, and as fur as that goes, we found some, only the law took it away. But what I want to say is that we know you have things to say that is not in your book, not only about treasure, but about a lot of things. And anyway, we want to see you, and the Mississippi, and Huck, and your folks, and have a visit.

Nobody knows that I'm writin' this letter, because they say here that you ain't real. But I know better, and Skeet does, and so I've made up my mind to try this letter. If you're real, write me and if you want us to come, say so, and we'll be there, if there's a way. Next to Skeet, I love you and Huck more than anybody in the world, barrin' near relatives, for I think you're brave and plucky, and square, as anybody would who reads your book. I want to meet Becky, too.

"Your Friend,
"Mitch Miller."

"Well," I said after readin' this, "when you goin' to send this?" "I have sent it," said Mitch. "This is a copy kept for you to see. Yes, sir, I've sent it, and here is Tom's letter to me."

He pulled a letter out all stamped and everything — stamped Hannibal, Missouri, and handed it to me to take the letter out my own self, which I did, and read:

"Dear Mitch: It's all right for you to come down here and we'll be glad to see you — although you can't depend much on Huck for he's in trouble all the time with his pap. The old man is lawin' with Judge Thatcher about Huck's money, and Huck ain't had any peace of mind since we found the treasure. Don't think I'm puttin' on airs, when I say that this findin' of treasure ain't what it's cracked up to be. You see I ain't got my own money either. Aunt Polly is my guardeen, and it's put away until I grow up and have some sense, as she says. By that time, maybe I won't know what to do with it, or we'll be dead or somethin'. You never can tell, and everything is so blamed uncertain. But if I can help you and Skeet any way, I'll do it, and so will

Huck. Yours is the first letter I ever got, because everybody I know lives here, and I'm glad to hear from you.
So come along, and if we can't put you up here, we'll
get the Widow Douglas to take you in. And maybe if
I can get you to give up this treasure huntin', which ain't
much after all, you'll want to join the gang I'm formin'
— that is if I really see that you and Skeet are the right
kind. I sign myself,

                              "Your Friend,
                                  "Tom Sawyer."

"There," said Mitch — "how's that? And to show
you it's Tom's writin', I've brought the book along.
Look here!" Mitch turned to where Tom wrote on the
shingle with blood, and sure enough the writin' was the
same. Any one could see it; and so Tom Sawyer was a
real person, and it was proved.

Then Mitch said: "Go out to your grandpa's and
stay a week. That'll give you time to get strong again.
I'm ready to start now, but you ain't. We may have
to walk miles and miles, and you must be able to keep
up a good pace; for while we can hop some rides now and
then, we'll have to do a lot of walkin'. And then we'll
have to sleep in barns, in hay-stacks, and everywheres
on the way, and pick up what we can eat by odd jobs,
maybe."

Says I, "I can get some money. My grandma will
pay me for helpin' her. And maybe I can have a couple
of dollars by the time I'm fit to go."

Mitch says: "Charley King has the agency for the
Springfield papers, and he's goin' to divy with me for
helpin' him deliver, and that way I can get some money
too. But shucks, as for that, we can turn tricks on the

way for money. All we need is hand-outs, and that's easy."

"Well, then," says I, "let me furnish the money. You just plan things out and wait for me."

Mitch caught somethin' in my voice, and he said, "What makes you say that? I'm square. I want to do my share on the money."

"Well," says I, "I don't like to have you goin' with Charley King. It don't seem the thing to me. His folks don't seem right to me; and he's older than you, and I'm afraid somethin' will happen. I have a funny feelin' about that boy and about George Heigold, too."

"Oh, you're just ticklish," said Mitch, "and if you're afeard they can win me away from you, don't think of it, for they can't, and no one can."

All this time I'd forgot something. Here we was plannin' to go to Hannibal in about a week, when it was clear out of the question, for it was gettin' close to court time, and we was subpoened, Mitch and me, to testify against Doc Lyon. It was clear crazy to think of goin' to Hannibal and gettin' back in time. And I'd made up my mind to stick it out — we couldn't run away for good. And if I had anything to say, I wasn't goin' to let Mitch slump on that. Here was a chance to get rid of a awful criminal, this Doc Lyon, and we could help, and it was our duty. Pa had said so. So I spoke up and says to Mitch, "You've forgot somethin', Mitch. We can't leave till this Doc Lyon matter is all fixed."

"It's fixed," said Mitch.

"How?" says I.

"Doc Lyon fixed it his own self. He killed hisself in jail while you was sick."

"What!" says I.

"Yep," says Mitch. "He's dead and buried, and we're out of the law, and I say let's keep out. Let's never be a witness to anything again. We ain't got time till we get this treasure. Do you promise?"

I said "yes."

Then Mitch took my hand and said, "A week from Saturday be down at the corner where Linkern got the line wrong, and I'll have everything ready, and we'll go."

So I promised, and Mitch said good-by and left.

CHAPTER XIII

I COULD hardly wait for Saturday to come, for there wasn't anything to do. And everywheres in the house I saw somethin' that made me think of Little Billie. There was his French harp, and the glass bank that Uncle Harvey had given him; and onct I went into a closet and saw his hat hangin' there yet, and I kept wonderin' if I had been a good brother to him always. Of course there was the time I wouldn't let him go when Old Bender's house was burned down, and that hurt me to think of it. But we did carry him on our hands, Mitch and me, one time from the river. And Mitch said he thought I'd been a good brother, and that Little Billie thought so too. Ma said she just couldn't live with Little Billie gone — Myrtle and me didn't answer, somehow. And one day I heard her singin' at the piano — she and pa had joined the town troupe to sing Pinafore. She was Little Buttercup, and pa was Dick Deadeye, and so they practiced together. And I always, to this day, think of Little Billie whenever I hear any one sing "The Nightingale Sighs for the Moon's Bright Rays." These things always get mixed together and stay mixed, so my ma says.

Well, Saturday came, and I went down to the square and found my grandpa on the corner, talkin' temperance to a man and sayin' that he'd seen slavery abolished and he hoped to live to see strong drink done away with, that it was sure to come, the questions were just alike; and that Linkern was against slavery and strong drink both, and if he was livin' he would be in this new fight. And this other man kept sayin', "you're right, you're right," and noddin' his head. So when my grandpa saw me, his eyes grew wonderful kind, and he said, "Son, we're goin' right away. Go put your things in the carriage. Your grandma is over at the store. Go over and see her." I went over and found her, and she bought me some jeans to work in and a blue shirt and some heavy shoes to walk through the briars and thickets in, and she said, "Now, we're ready. Go and tell your grandpa." I went back and grandpa was talkin' to another man, about temperance, and sayin' to him that he'd seen slavery abolished and he expected to live to see hard drink done away with. I told him grandma was ready; and he said to go back and tell grandma to go to the harness shop and wait, he had to come there for a halter, and he'd pick us up there. I went back and told her and we went to the harness shop and waited. But grandpa didn't come; and finally grandma said to go out and see what was the matter, and I did, and found grandpa comin' out of the bank. It looked like we'd never get started. But he said, "Come on, Son, we must hurry. It may rain. My darlin', it looks like it." So I thought we were off at last. And just then a man came up and spoke to him. And they began to talk and I stood by restless and gettin' tired. They began to talk temperance, too. And grandpa told him that he'd seen slavery abolished and he hoped to live to see hard drink done away with. And the man said it would come; and then they talked about the corn crop and things, and finally grandpa got away from him and we started for the harness shop. But when we got up to the big store, grandpa says, " Bless me, I've forgot my spectacles at the jeweler's." And he turned around and trotted back. I didn't know whether to foller him or to wait, or to go on to the harness shop. I decided to foller him to keep him from gettin' into more talks, if I could. I suppose he stopped or was stopped a dozen times to talk; and he and the jeweler had a long talk. Mitch and me never wasted time this a way. I couldn't understand it.

Then we got over to the hitchin' rack, and got into the carriage and started for the harness shop. Grandma was fussed and began to scold, and grandpa just laughed and said, " Hey! hey!" and went for his halter. He and the harness maker had a considerable talk, and at last we got started.

By this time I was tired clear out and fell asleep before we got to the fair grounds and slept until we got to the hill where you first see the farm house. And then when we drove into the lot, my Uncle Henry came to take the horses. And I wondered and asked, "Where's Willie Wallace?" "He's gone to work on the railroad. He's a brakeman now," said my uncle. My heart sunk clear down, for I had expected to go fishin' with him, and ride around the country while he was haulin' corn. And it made me sad to think he was gone for good, and maybe at this very minute was in some noisy, wicked place, like Peoria, with railroad men, conductors and such. Anyway, he was gone, and they had no one in his place. And grandma said, "It's a great mistake. He'll get killed, or get into bad company. It's not a good thing to leave home and your place and go gallivantin' around the country on the cars." But it seemed he wasn't so far away, after all. He was on the C. P. which came through Atterberry, and I was bettin' if we went there some day when the train came through we could see him in the caboose, or runnin' on top of the cars, or couplin' and sayin' "back her up," or motionin' to go ahead.

You can bet that grandma started to get me well. I had the softest bed you ever see, and the best things to eat, and a horse to ride, and we went visitin' around to the neighbors, and over to old Cy McDoel's who was dyin' that summer and had been in bed a long while. He was about ninety. I saw and heard my grandpa say to Cy, "I seen slavery abolished, and I expect to live to see hard drink done away with." And Cy said, "You will, but I won't. But it makes no difference. The Lord will have His own way. Blessed be the name of the Lord." The flies was awful and every now and then Cy's granddaughter came in to fan the flies off him — but they came right back.

By Wednesday it seemed I'd been there a month. I had made kites and done about everything, and I began to think of Saturday, when I'd see Mitch. So on Thursday I said to grandma that I had to go by Saturday, and she says, "Your popie said you was to stay all this month. You must get well, and besides I want you here with me."

I began to see I was in for it, and what would Mitch say? He would be waitin' for me on the corner where Linkern got the line wrong, and what would he think? There was nothing to do but to run away or do somethin' so they wouldn't want me any more. And I didn't want to do that, but I pretty near stumbled into it. That afternoon I went out into the work house and there I found all kinds of paint, red, white, blue and green. So

I began to paint pictures. Then I took to paintin' signs. I got a nice board and painted a beer keg on it with a glass under the faucet and beer runnin' in it, all white and foamy. Then I painted some letters, "Billiards and Beer." It was a dandy sign — as good as you see in town.

There was an outdoor cellar in the yard, and over the cellar a shed that you could see from the road; so I nailed the sign up on the shed and stood off and looked at it. I wasn't thinkin' — I wasn't tryin' to do a thing. But it looked so funny considerin' that grandpa said that he'd seen slavery abolished and he'd live to see hard drink done away with too. And I just laughed. Grandma came out and said, "What you laughin' at, Skeet?" Says I, "At the chickens." "Here," she says, "don't you feed them poor dumb creatures red flannel again. Have you?" "No'm," I said. "Well, if you do, I'll flax you," and she went into the kitchen.

That very afternoon a peddler came into the yard. He had an oilcloth pack full of tablecloths, napkins, towels, suspenders, lead pencils, laces, overalls, mirrors, combs — a lot of things. And he threw his pack down and opened it up. Grandpa was carryin' slop to the pigs. It was awful hot; you couldn't hardly breathe — except when you got in front of the cellar door. Grandpa had no use for peddlers and never bought nothin' of 'em, and he kept answerin' the peddler short and carryin' slop, so as to keep away from hearin' him ask: "Any napkins, any handkerchiefs, any combs?" Grandpa kept sayin', "Nope, nope, nope." I was standing there and all at once I saw the peddler glue his eye on the sign "Billiards and Beer" — so I thought somethin' was goin' to happen, and went into the dinin' room and looked out of the window. Then the peddler folded up

his pack and strapped it, and turned to grandpa and
said, " I'll take a beer."

Grandpa didn't understand him. He didn't know
about the sign, and if the peddler had said, "I'll take a
set of plush furniture," or "Give me a barrel of coal
oil," it would have meant just as much to him. Grandpa
looked at him as if he was crazy. "Do you keep it real

"I'll Take a Beer"

cold?" said the peddler. "What?" said my grandpa.
"Why, the beer. Because that's the way I like it. And
come to think of it, I'll take a bucket. It's hotter'n
blazes and my throat is caked with dust."

Then grandpa thought that the peddler was mad and
was mockin' him because he didn't buy anything, and
that the peddler had heard about his temperance work
and was tryin' to be insultin'. So he said, "If you're
thirsty, here's plenty of slops."

So then the peddler flew all to pieces. "Well, this is
what I'd like to know. I want you to tell me. I want
to know why you make fools of people. I want to know
what's the matter with me. You won't buy of me, and
you won't sell to me. And I'd like to know what I've
done. I'm a man, the same as you. And you've got
beer to sell. And you have no right to discriminate,
even if I was a nigger, which I'm not. I've been respectful to you, and I don't deserve this here treatment. And
I won't stand it. You've either got the right to sell
it, or you ain't; and if you ain't I'll have the law on you,
and if you have, I want the beer — that's what I want.
I speak right out what I think. And what right have
you to put up a sign like that and attract people from
the road if you didn't mean to sell it?" And he pointed
to the sign.

"What sign?" said grandpa, comin' around and lookin'
up and seein' it. "Tut, tut," said grandpa, completely
dazed like. I run up-stairs and hid, but I could hear.
Then grandma came out and said: "Look here! That's
just a prank of our grandson. It's too bad! It's a shame.
Sit down and rest and I'll bring you somethin'."
Grandpa went off sommers; and pretty soon grandma
came out with a glass clinkin' with ice, and after a bit
I heard the peddler say, "Is this blackberry wine?"
And grandma said, "Yes." And the peddler said: "Well,
it's better'n beer, and I thank ye. You've saved my life.
And if you advertised this here, you couldn't make
enough of it." Then the peddler seemed to grow bolder
somehow and finally he came back to the wine and he
said, "I suppose your husband don't know you keep
this." Grandma says: "There's certain medicines I
believe in — for people that need 'em. And now you feel

well enough to go on your way, and I wish you good luck."

So the peddler went off down the road.

And pretty soon grandma came upstairs and said: "Your grandpa is awful vexed. He'd most pull your hair. And you'd better stay here, and I'll bring some supper to you after a bit, and we'll let this quiet down."

"Well, this is Thursday," says I, "and I'm goin' Saturday anyway. And suppose I go to-night — I can walk in." Grandma says: "Your popie is comin' in the morning on the way to Havaner, and you stay and see him. And if he says you can go, why all right. Or maybe he'll take you to Havaner with him." A thought went through my head! Why not go to Havaner and get the lay of the land, see the steamboats and get ready to go to Hannibal. So grandma brought me my supper, and I went to bed dreamin' of the steamboats.

CHAPTER XIV

WHILE I was at my grandpa's this time, my Aunt Melissa and Uncle Lemuel came to visit on their way to Ohio. They lived in Iowa sommers and he was a preacher and awful smart. He had been married before and his wife died, and then he married my aunt. My pa said a preacher would never do without a wife, especially if he was a Methodist. Besides being lonely, my pa said Uncle Lemuel thought Aunt Melissa would inherit, and of course the time comes when a preacher can't preach and must either go to a preacher's home and be supported or else have help from his wife, because they can't lay up much.

Well, Uncle Lemuel was awful smart. He didn't know Greek or Latin, but he had read the translations and he knew the Bible from A to Z and he could sing in a deep voice, and when he preached he made you scared and ashamed. They petted me a lot — both Aunt Melissa and Uncle Lemuel. They held me on their laps and stroked my head, and asked me about Sunday School and whether I really loved Jesus or only just said so.

There was always a lot goin' on when they visited and I sat and watched. In the first place, when they would come they had a lot of bags, carpet bags and boxes, and you had to be awful particular of 'em, and the hired man had to carry 'em to the house and Aunt Melissa would say be careful, and if he dropped anything, there was an awful scare about it. This time they got here just before dinner; and grandma had a big dinner for 'em — lots of fried chicken and mashed potatoes, and you ought to see Uncle Lemuel eat, and Aunt Melissa, too. You'd almost think they didn't have food in Iowa.

But first I noticed that grandpa always kind of shriveled when Uncle Lemuel came. His voice was high compared to Uncle Lemuel's, besides he didn't know so much, not even about the Bible, though grandpa hadn't read anything else for 50 years except the prohibition paper. Well, of course grandpa gave up to him the sayin' of grace, and Uncle Lemuel said it in a voice that made the dishes kind of tremble, just like low thunder, and we all

UNCLE LEMUEL

looked down, except me. I looked out of one eye a little to see him, and watch my grandma, who was lookin' down of course, but with a look which said: "this is all very well, but here's the dinner which I got and which is to be et. There's real things here before us." Then after grace Uncle Lemuel would tell stories about darkies and things — no swear words, sometimes kind of a funny point, and grandpa would laugh, sometimes the hired man would laugh, sometimes grandma would — not much though. And Aunt Melissa would just smile — she'd heard it before, maybe. Then grandpa would ask Uncle Lemuel questions about politics and church and things, and ask him what he thought would happen. And Uncle Lemuel would talk and grandpa would say, "Yes," "Well, well," "You don't say so," and things like that sometimes, awful surprised. And all the time Uncle Lemuel would be eatin', and of course, bein' a son-in-law, he could have as much as he liked; and they kept passin' the chicken to him until the bones was just piled around his plate.

This time they didn't bring their boy Archie. They had just one child, and he was supposed to be awful bad, but they was givin' him a Christian rearin' and expected to make a good man of him. My grandma said that one time when they was here he forgot to say his prayers and sassed Aunt Melissa when she spoke to him about it, and that Uncle Lemuel made her get a strap and strop him. Uncle Lemuel stood at the head of the stair and said to Aunt Melissa, "A little more, Melissa, a little harder." And so they whipped him good, and after that he prayed and thanked God for parents that wouldn't let him forget his prayers but made him say 'em. And onct there was a Dutch boy that came over to play with Archie and Archie got him out in the ice house and got a rope around his neck and pulled him up. Archie was playin' hangin' and this Dutch boy was the criminal and was bein' hanged for a crime. And grandma kind of heard a noise or suspected somethin', so she came into the wood house and found this here Dutch boy clawin' at the rope and kind of purple in the face, and Archie standin' by pretendin' to hold a watch and be the sheriff. Well, this time Uncle Lemuel whipped Archie with the strap; and after that they made him pray, and put him in a dark

room and kept him on bread and water for a day. Then
they let him out and he kissed his pa and his ma and said
he loved 'em and loved God and was all right now and
would never commit another sin while he lived.

But to come back to eatin' chicken, if you've ever
seen bricks piled, kind a thrown down in a pile around
a mortar box, that's the way the chicken bones looked
around Uncle Lemuel's plate; and all the time there
was a lot of talk about the evil of intemperance and the
curse of strong drink, and grandpa said that he'd seen
slavery abolished, and the time would come when
strong drink would be abolished too.

Then in the afternoon we generally had singin' and
music; and Uncle Lemuel played the piano and sang
"Swing Low, Sweet Chariot" in a terrible deep voice,
and all the rest joined as well as they could. And then
after while everybody would get to cryin' and Uncle
Lemuel would say that beyond the weepin' and the
wailin' here there was a land of pure delight where we
would all be. And Uncle Lemuel would put his hand
on my head and ask me if I didn't believe it, and I said
yes, I did, though so far as my thoughts went, I didn't
know much about it, and I kept thinkin' of heaven as a
place where dead folks suddenly made alive went around
in their night-gowns not doin' very much, except just
smilin' sweet on each other and saying soft words.

Grandma always seemed kind of apart at these times,
as if she believed everything maybe, and approved of
it, but kind of as if there was other things which she
had to think of and which kept her from takin' part
as much as Uncle Lemuel and Aunt Melissa, and even
grandpa, who didn't have anything else to do. For
grandma always had the meals to get and the cows to

I

milk, and so much business like that to run; and she never shed any tears except when she was really sayin' good-by to some one, or maybe when she'd get to talkin' about some of the children which had died and which she loved so much.

Of course there was always prayers at night, and in the morning prayers, and readin' from the Bible, which Uncle Lemuel carried on, grandpa standin' back for him. And I came in for a lot of talk about bein' a good boy and man and never touchin' liquor or tobacco, or dancin' or goin' to bad theaters and such like. And Uncle Lemuel talked to me about this treasure huntin', for he'd heard it somehow. And he said to me to lay up treasure in heaven where moths don't come nor thieves; and he said that riches was nothin' because they could be lost so easy; but if a man improved his character and learnt things, he couldn't lose 'em, and no one could take your knowledge away from you, and you couldn't lose it. And onct, while he was talkin' this away, he was tryin' to remember the place in the Bible where there was a text he wanted to say to me, and he couldn't remember the place; and he asked grandpa where it was and grandpa couldn't remember, for you see grandpa was pretty old. Grandpa had been kind of dozin' while Uncle Lemuel was talkin' to me, but he woke up when Uncle Lemuel asked him where that text was and when grandpa couldn't remember, he says to Uncle Lemuel: "I can't remember like I used to, Lemuel, and a lot of it has gone out of my mind, which I remember when somebody says it to me, maybe, but except for that, it's gone. And sometimes I don't know folks that I've known always, and I forget my specs, and leave my bank book in the wrong place, and make mistakes adding up figures; for you see, as the good book says, things change with us, the grinders become fewer, we lose our teeth; those that looks out of the window are darkened, and we have to get stronger specs; and the truth is we become children again, and if we had to live our life over from that point, we'd have to learn a lot of things over again, if not everything." And Uncle Lemuel said it was true, and for that reason it proved God's mercy and love to take people to 'im when they got this a way and not let 'em go on forever stumbling about in this sad world.

Well, so it would be after a few days that Uncle Lemuel and Aunt Melissa would have to go; for they always had important things to do in teaching religion; and Uncle Lemuel had to lecture, and this time they was goin' as far east as Ohio. And after singin' "God be with us till we Meet Again" and prayers and everybody cryin' but grandma, they got ready to go. Grandpa come up with the carriage and the white horses and grandma was in the kitchen makin' up a box of lunch — fried chicken and brown bread and preserves and cake, because Uncle Lemuel didn't like the lunch counters along the way. And finally grandma came with the box, and Uncle Lemuel and Aunt Melissa was standin' by the door waitin' and ready. So she handed the box to 'em and kissed 'em, and Aunt Melissa cried some more and so they went.

I stood at the door with grandma until they drove off, and then grandma said to me: "Go put on your boots, Skeet, and we'll go over into the woods and look for flowers. I need a change." So we did, and grandma acted like a wild young girl, laughin' and tellin' stories and makin' a lovely bouquet.

CHAPTER XV

THE next mornin' when I got down to breakfast, everybody had et and grandpa had gone down the road where the tenant was buildin' a fence. So I took my kite and went way into the middle of the pasture and sent her up. Then I lay on the grass and watched her sail and drift and looked over at the Mason County Hills, that seemed so mysterious and quiet and never ending. By and by I thought I heard somebody callin' me — and there was. It was grandma. So I hollered back and drew in my kite, and went to the house. And there was my pa. He looked so powerful, and his voice was so deep, and he was so full of fun. You'd never thought he was the same man who was beside hisself over Little Billie. And he was awful glad to see me, and took me on his knee and pulled out a knife he had brought me for a present. Of course grandpa wouldn't say anything about that sign in front of my pa — it warn't the place and didn't fit in. But, anyway, grandpa seemed himself again. So I sat down and listened to 'em talk.

Before they had got very far my grandpa said he'd seen slavery abolished and the time warn't far off when hard drink would be done away with. I was eyein' my pa close, for I knew he drank a beer now and then, and I wanted to see what he'd say. But he didn't say nothin'. He just looked calm, and as grandpa went right on talkin', it would have been interruptin' if my pa did say anything. So he got over that place in the conversation without any trouble. Later, just before dinner, I saw grandma give pa a drink of blackberry wine and take a little herself. She came from a different part of Kentucky from what grandpa did. And yet they lived happy. It was because she was so smart and like a piece of oiled leather that bends and don't crack.

Well, as I said, I sat listenin' to my pa and grandpa talk — awful interestin', too. Pa was tellin' about "Pinafore"; but grandpa kind o' smiled in a forced way, because he didn't believe in shows. But pretty soon it came out that Joe Rainey had been killed the night before, and Temple Scott had killed him, which boarded at their house. And so I knew there was another case. And I said to myself, it's lucky I was here, for if I'd been in town, most likely Mitch and me would have been around sommers and been witnesses, and got into another tangle, to keep us from goin' to see Tom Sawyer.

It was this a way, as pa told it. Joe Rainey was drinkin' and he and Temple Scott was always the best of friends, but when he was drinkin' he always quarreled with Scott and threatened him. Then my pa says: "His threats came to nothin'. He wouldn't harm a child. He's threatened me a hundred times. I never paid any attention to him. Every one knows he was harmless."

They were practicin' "Pinafore" at Joe Rainey's house — my pa, my ma, and just as my pa was singin':

The merry, merry maiden, the merry, merry maiden,
The merry, merry maiden and the tar,

all of a sudden they heard a shot, and then another shot, and somebody opened the door, and there was

Joe Rainey lyin' on the porch, almost dead — unconscious, and bleedin'. And Temple Scott had stood his
ground and said that Rainey had threatened to kill him,
and had drawn his pistol first, and that he shot him in
self-defense. My grandpa interrupted to talk about the
sin of drink and what it makes people do. Then pa went
on to say that they searched Joe Rainey's pocket and
couldn't find his pistol; that later they searched the
house and his office and couldn't find his pistol, and the
wonder was where it was. And pa said he didn't believe
he had a pistol, at least with him at the time. But Mrs.
Rainey said that her husband had come into the house
earlier in the evening and got the pistol. But pa said
that Mrs. Rainey was too sweet on Temple, and he didn't
believe her, and he intended to prosecute Temple Scott
as hard as he could and hang him. Then he said that this
broke up the practicin' of " Pinafore," that Mrs. Rainey
was goin' to play Josephine, but now that her husband
was killed, she couldn't. That they all went home, and
that the town was full of talk over it, and where the pistol
was if Joe Rainey ever had one.

Well, Joe Rainey had died about one o'clock that
mornin', beggin' every one not to let him fall asleep for
fear he wouldn't wake up no more. They had give him
ether or somethin' and so he kept gettin' drowsier and
drowsier, and finally died in his sleep.

So my pa and grandpa talked till noon — most wonderful talk; and then we had dinner and grandma told
more funny stories than you ever heard, and had the
best time in the world. And after dinner, grandpa
hitched up the horses and drove pa to Atterberry to
catch the train for Havaner. But pa wouldn't take me.
He says, "No, sir, you stay here and get well, and mind

your grandma and help her. If you don't, I'll whale
you. And I'll come for you a week from Saturday,
maybe."

That settled that, I was afraid. "Well, then," I said,
"will you tell Mitch that I'll be back a week from Saturday?" He said he would, and I made up my mind to it.

What do you suppose, when we got to Atterberry,
there was Willie Wallace in charge of a freight train
which had side-tracked for the passenger goin' to Havaner. You can't imagine how funny it seemed to see
him talkin' to the conductor and everything; and how
funny it seemed that I knowed him so well, since I had
seen him plow and drive a team and all that on the farm.

"How do you like it?" says I to Willie.

"No more farm for me," says Willie.

"Ain't you afeard? Ain't it dangerous?"

"Yes, it's dangerous," says he. "But look at the
pay. And then look at the fun. One night it's Springfield, the next night Peoria — always somethin' new."

Just then the passenger train whistled, and Willie
got up and began to motion to the engineer on his train.
I went back to the platform and said good-by to pa.
And then we drove back to the farm.

CHAPTER XVI

WHEN we got back to the farm, who do you suppose was there? My ma and Myrtle. She said she was just tired stayin' alone all the time — that pa was always away; and now that Little Billie was dead, she couldn't stand it. She said she never seed such a town as Petersburg was, that she had half a mind to go back to Boston where she was born and raised. That she didn't believe there was such characters in the whole world as Doc Lyon and dozens of others in Petersburg, Joe Pink, and the hoodlums and roughs, and she was afeard all the time some of 'em would kill pa for bein' States Attorney. That it was just one murder after another, that even she'd lost confidence in Mrs. Rainey, who had been her friend, and couldn't understand the talk about Joe Rainey having a pistol when there was no pistol. Then she said that's one part of the town; and the other part was narrow as a knife blade, that they were talkin' of churchin' Mr. Miller and drivin' him out of the pulpit and for nothin' except sayin' that God was in everything, and that there wasn't room enough in the world for anything but God. Sometimes Mr. Miller when he was preachin', got to dreamin' and would wander way off. He had done this when talkin' about God and give hisself away — that's what they said. And what was he goin' to do with so many children and nothin' saved because he never made nothin', and nothin' to do if

he couldn't preach? Grandpa said, "Well, where does
that doctrine put old Satan?" And ma says, "Of
course it puts him out of the world, which I don't believe;
there's too much sin in the world to believe that; but
anyway a man has a right to his opinions without bein'
persecuted for 'em."

All the time Myrtle was leanin' against ma, just like
a cat, actin', I thought. She did make me terrible mad
sometimes. Grandpa couldn't see through her. He
petted her and went out and saddled a horse and put her
on it and led the horse around the lot for 'bout an hour,
right in the sun. And then she came in and began to
honey around grandma and get things. I saw the game
was spoiled for me, and wanted the time to go by so I
could get away, or for somethin' to happen. Then about
eleven o'clock grandma came into the settin' room with
apples to peel, and ma helped her and they began to
talk — and it was wonderful to listen, for it was about
Mitch and Zueline. Ma said she'd never seed such children, such a boy as Mitch, that he would be a musician
or a poet like Longfellow when he grew up; that he was
dreamin' all the time and believed in fairy stories, and
made everything real to hisself. Then she said that
Mitch thought so much of Zueline that it was enough
to scare a body; that if anything happened to her Mitch
would go out of his head, and if they was separated it
would kill him, and she thought they would be separated.
That Mrs. Hasson thought of takin' a trip, and takin'
Zueline, but was keepin' it quiet. Grandma said it was
silly for two children to act that a way, or at least for
Mitch to act that a way. Zueline warn't doin' anything
except just to be Zueline to Mitch — she wasn't as
much in love with Mitch as he was with her.

Then grandpa came in and said we'd all go to Bob-town the next day, that his spring wagon was done and we'd go over and get it. It was an awful ways, eighteen miles at least, and we'd have to start by six o'clock in order to get there and get back, and take a lunch to eat on the way. I suppose I had heard as much about Bob-town as any place in the world, but never seen it. It was just in a straight line from the porch at grandpa's, past Spotty Milt Stith's place, and just in the place between the woods and where the sky came down be-yond. So the next mornin' we was off — grandpa and ma settin' in the front seat of the carriage; and me, grandma and Myrtle in the back seat. And ma began right away to talk about Petersburg, they agreed about hard drink and a lot of things.

But grandpa said that he'd been in the war and had seen two, and he'd like to see war abolished with slavery and hard drink. He was in the Black Hawk War, but that wasn't much; but the Mexican War was bad and warn't necessary, and was unjust, even Linkern thought so, and had stirred up a lot of hate. And he said the Civil War had left things bad. It had killed off a lot of fine young men, and herded toughs into places like Petersburg and stirred up all kinds of hate and bad feelin's, and made people dishonest and tricky and care-less and lazy — and we'd have to stand the consequences for years to come in politics and everything. And he said the way to avoid war was the same as a man would avoid fightin' or killin' another man — you could do it mostly by usin' your mind and bein' a civilized being and not standin' too much on your pride and all that. But if you couldn't avoid it, then fight and fight hard.

It was pretty near eleven o'clock and we came in sight

of a white steeple and white houses, right amongst green
trees — and sure enough it was Bobtown. I was so
excited I could hardly stand it. And I said: "It's a
downright shame that Mitch ain't here. He never saw
Bobtown, and he's there in Petersburg waitin' for me,
and here I am havin' this wonderful trip." We were
just in a little grove, and grandpa stopped and unreined
the horses and fed 'em and said, "We'll have our lunch
here." "Oh," says I, "let's go on to Bobtown first."
Grandpa laughed, for he knew I was wild to go on.
But he said, "By and by." So we spread the table-cloth
on the grass and had the lunch — and it was wonderful,
fried chicken and blackberry pie and about everything.
Then we drove into Bobtown. Here was a drug store,
and a post-office and a billiard parlor, and a saloon kept
by Porky Jim Thomas, grandpa said; and a lot of white
houses, and a big store, and this wagon shop which was
also a blacksmith shop. We separated now. Grandma
and ma and Myrtle went to the store, and grandpa and
me to the wagon shop.

The wagon maker was a big man with bushy hair and
he was tickled to death to see my grandpa. The wagon
was all done, all except puttin' in a few bolts. It shone
like a lookin' glass, all varnished up with pretty pictures
on the sides, and the man said it would be ready in an
hour. So grandpa said he'd go to see a man about the
temperance work, and I could go with him or stay
around. So I stayed to see the wagon finished.

I hadn't noticed a man sittin' on a bench in the shop
and whittlin'; but when grandpa was gone, he said to
the blacksmith, "Ain't that Squire Kirby?" (they called
grandpa squire because he had been Justice of the Peace
onct); and the blacksmith said "yes"; and the man said:

"I suppose he's sincere. I suppose so, but that ain't the whole story. He gets used by people who ain't sincere, who want law about temperance, but don't want it about somethin' else. It's a hell of a country," he went on, "everybody is talkin' about law and about enforcin' the law, and everybody is breakin' the law himself. Take Porky Jim Thomas, they make an awful fuss about his sellin' to habituals or anything, and look at it: who sells Porky Jim adulterated stuff, who allows it to be sold to him? Are the revenue agents obeyin' the law? No, they ain't. Go right down the list. Congress don't obey the law — they don't obey the constitution. Yet they're always talkin' law and denouncin' law breakers. Do the judges obey the law? No, they don't — they talk about it and make other folks obey what they say is the law. And everywhere you go you hear about law breakers from people breakin' the law themselves — they're all breakin' it, and them that's highest is breakin' it most — and it's just like ants climbin' over each other — that's what it's like — and it ain't worth a damn. Look what the city folks do to the farmers. And take the mine owners — they don't obey the law, they don't prop their ceilin's and protect their men as the law says. And now they're goin' to strike over at Springfield, and you hear talk of the law and they're goin' to call out the guards. And look at me — losin' my farm through the law — just look anywhere you want and you'll see the same thing — everybody hollerin' law and nobody obeyin' it himself."

"Lem," said the blacksmith, "you've been mad ever since the war."

"Wal, ain't I got a right to be? Here I was just a young feller and hated slavery and loved liberty, and I was one of the first to volunteer. Yes, sir, I went right into Petersburg when Cap Estil was recruitin' and joined the army and me not more'n seventeen, and all because I wanted to help free the country and put down rebellion, and serve God. Yes, that's what a boy says to hisself, ' God and my country.' You get into kind of a religion. Wal, what happened? They treat a soldier worse'n a dog — they feed you like a dog and sleep you like a dog. And they order you in danger worse'n a dog. What in hell are you, anyway? Here you are, we'll say, with a couple of hundred, and the captain thinks that by sacrificing a couple of hundred, he can do somethin', turn a certain trick. It's like checkers, you make a sacrifice to get into the king's row and come back stronger and clean up the board. That's how I got it. They ordered us in when it was death to go, and I got it through the lung, and here I am, no good to this here day."

"Lem," says the blacksmith, "you talk like a democrat."

"Wal, I ain't no democrat. I ain't nothin'. How can a man be anything? Look at what they did. Look at the way the stay-at-homes made money. Look at the grabs in the country, look at the money scandals, look at the poor, look at the fellers goin' around in the name of the army gettin' themselves elected to office. Just look at the country. Look at me with just enough pension to keep body and soul together, and tryin' to grub out a little farm. Why, look here, if the next generation knew what we know about war, how they get it up, and how they get the young fellers into it, and what it means after they get into it, you couldn't get 'em into a war. That's the way to stop war. Pass the word along,

so the young fellers that can fight will know what they're
a takin' a hold of — and they won't fight. You can't
burn a child that knows the fire. These here pot-bellies
that sit in banks, and these here loud-mouthed orators
that make speeches and say they wished they could go
to war, it's their only regret that they can't go, and die

LIKE A PIECE OF LICORICE

with the flag in their hands — these fellers, damn 'em,
can't make any headway if the boys are on to the game.
And, by God, furst thing you know they ain't anybody
to do the fightin' but the pot-bellies and the orators
who want to die but are too old to carry a gun, and so go
around lamentin' their age, the furst thing you know,
nobody is left but 'em to fight. And then there won't
be no war, because they wouldn't fight. They are too

careful of their precious selves, and too afraid of hell, and have got over believin' in God, or country, except the price of corn and cotton, and so that ends war. And that's the way to end it, pass the word along."

So he went on talkin' and the blacksmith was makin' a rod and he took it out of the forge and put it on the anvil and it sputtered sparks, and he pounded it around, and finally he took a chisel and cut off a piece, and I watched it grow from dull red till it got black and looked like a piece of licorice. So I went and picked it up. Gee! but it just cooked my fingers, and I yelled. "Thar's your lesson," says Lem — "remember it. Don't take hold of a hot thing till it gets cold. Thar's your lesson, remember that as long as you live."

But I was cryin' and my grandpa came in and when he heard Lem talk, he said Lem had been drinkin', poor feller, and was another victim of the awful curse of drink. So he took me to the drug store and got somethin', and by and by I was better and so we drove home to the farm.

CHAPTER XVII

IT was only Tuesday, and the days just dragged by. It seemed Saturday was a year off, when I was to see Mitch. I was out in the front yard about nine o'clock and all the rest was in the house. My uncle came along and began to sharpen a scythe on the grinder and I was turnin' it for him. I was teasin' him to go to the river and fish and camp out over night. He said it was too hot, and besides we needed another man, and Willie Wallace was gone, and he couldn't get Bud Entrekin to go until he'd hauled some corn. By and by he got the scythe sharp and went away to cut weeds. While I was standin' there wonderin' what to do, I heard a low whistle and looked over the fence and there was Mitch. He didn't look very gay. He was covered with dust, had been walkin' since early mornin'. He scrooched down behind the fence and whispered to me to come over into the orchard. We got down in the grass by a tree, first lookin' for snakes, and then Mitch said: "How much money you got?" I said, I thought I could get two dollars anyway, and he said, "That's bully, I've got 80 cents and that's enough." "What you goin' to do, Mitch, you're not goin' to see Tom now, are you?" Says he: "The time has come. Go get your money and we'll start right now."

He almost scared me, he was so quick and earnest. Then he said, "I've got somethin' on my mind, a good deal on my mind. The time has come to go. There's nothin' left but Old Salem, and we can finish that any time — and let's go now and see Tom before anything else happens. Pretty soon the summer'll be over, and things keep happenin'. We must go now."

So he made me go to the house for my money. I had to ask grandma for it, and at first she wouldn't give it to me. She said I'd lose it. But I teased her till she went to her closet and gave it to me. Then said she: "You never let a body alone when you start. So here it is, and if you lose it — you lose it."

I went back to the tree in the orchard where Mitch was. Then we walked clear to the back of the orchard, clumb the rail fence, walked through the meadow a roundabout way and came to the road on the other side of the Tate farm. So here we struck out for Atterberry, so as to walk the railroad to Havaner. We thought we could make Oakford before night.

When we got fairly started Mitch said, "Something terrible has happened to me, Skeet — it's terrible."

"What?" says I.

"I can't talk about it now," says Mitch. "By and by I can, maybe. Of course I'll tell you — I must tell some one. But it's that made me come out here and see you, and not wait for Saturday. I just had to see you; and it seemed the time had just come for us to go to see Tom."

I says: "Well, Mitch, you know me, and if I can do anything, you know I'll do it. And maybe you'd better tell me right now."

"Well," says Mitch, "there's more'n one thing to tell — and both of 'em had somethin' to do with me comin' to-day. I couldn't stand the town another minute. I had to get away."

K

So we walked on and didn't get a lift or anything, and about eleven we came to Atterberry. We went into the store to get a bottle of pop, and while we was there, the train whistled, and the store-keeper says, "That's number 2. She's on time."

You never see such luck. We went out and the freight train pulled in and there was Willie Wallace. Well, he was that glad to see me. Here he was with gloves on and a cap with a silver label which said "Brakeman," and he was the happiest man you ever see.

I began to think what to say. We wanted to ride, but where was we goin', and did our folks know it? If we told him we was runnin' away to see Tom Sawyer, maybe he wouldn't let us on the train. So I began to play safe. I told him Mitch and me was goin' to Havaner to see my pa who was there, and come back with him to-morrow. Then I took out my two dollars and showed him, and says, "That's for my fare, and Mitch has money, too." Willie Wallace says: "You don't need no fare — just crawl up in the cupola of the caboose, and it will be all right. I owe your grandpap a lot for what he did for me in times past — and I'll pay part of it by lettin' you ride."

Then Willie walked away to go into the depot; and Mitch says, "Derned if I'm not proud of you, Skeet. That was a bully whack — and we've struck it rich. Our luck has turned at last."

We climbed up into the cupola and took seats, swingin' seats they was — and we could see all over the country — clean down to the woods where the river was, and over the fields far away. And pretty soon we was off, goin' like mad.

"What do you think of this?" says I.

"Why, Skeet," says Mitch, "did Tom Sawyer ever have anything like this? He never did. And come to think of it, was there a railroad in Tom's town? He never speaks of one. And nobody ever goes anywhere, except to Coonville, which maybe was as far from Tom's town

WILLIE WALLACE LETS US RIDE

as Atterberry from your grandpa's farm. Say, this is wonderful."

And Mitch took off his hat and let the wind blow through his sweaty hair. It was a wonderful day, and here we was, whizzin' right through the country, lookin' down on the fields, and goin' so fast that blackbirds flyin' alongside of us got way behind and couldn't keep up. Then we could whirl around in our chairs and look through the windows of the cupola all around the country.

We got to Oakford by and by and looked down on the men and boys standing by the depot, their hands in their pockets, chewin' tobacco, whittlin', jostlin' each other, laughin' and all that. Then the conductor came out of the depot with tissue papers in his hand and gave the signal and we started off. At Kilburn we did some switchin', put on a car with cattle in it. And here the conductor saw us for the first time.

He started to come up in the cupola and the first thing he says was, "Fares, please." "How much?" says I. "Where you goin'?" says he. "To Havaner," I says. "Where did you get on?" "At Atterberry," I says. I began to look for Willie Wallace, but he warn't anywhere around. Then the conductor says, "One dollar." I pulled a dollar out and handed it to him. Then he turned to Mitch and says, "You goin' to Havaner, too?" Mitch says, "Yes, sir." "One dollar, please," says the conductor. Mitch didn't have it — he only had 80 cents. So I gave my other dollar to the conductor, and he climbed into the cupola and stayed a bit and then climbed down and went away sommers.

Mitch says, "Well, that about cleans us out. We've got just 80 cents now between us. I thought Willie Wallace was your friend."

"He is," says I, "but I never met this here conductor before."

"It looks like it," says Mitch. "And now who knows what this will do to us? Suppose we have to pay our fare on the boat? That means we'll have to lay over long enough in Havaner to earn the money. One thing sometimes leads to another."

Just then Willie Wallace came through the caboose, and the train stopped. I looked out and saw we was alongside a corn-crib — nothin' else; but we began to back on to a switch, and pretty soon stopped. And now it was so still that you could hear the crickets chirp in the grass. It was a lonely country here — flat and sandy. Mitch and I got down and went to the back platform to see what Willie Wallace was doin'. He was standin' by the switch. And pretty soon the passenger train came whizzin' by. And what do you suppose? There stood pa on the back platform of the last car, smokin' a cigar and talkin' to a man.

We backed up and started on. Willie Wallace came into the caboose. Here we was in a pickle. If I complained to Willie Wallace about the conductor takin' two dollars for our fare, I was afraid he'd say, "Look here, what's your pa doin' on that train goin' back to Petersburg? You ain't goin' to Havaner to meet him — you're runnin' off — that's what you are. And I'll put you off here and you can walk back, or I'll take you to Havaner and give you over to the police." So I was afraid and I began to edge.

Says I : "What time does that train get to Petersburg, Willie?"

"About an hour from here," says he.

"Where does it come from?"

"Peoria."

"Does it come through Havaner?"

"Why, of course it does; why?"

"Because," says I, "I thought I saw a friend of my pa's standin' on the back platform."

"Who?" says Willie.

"Well, you don't know him," says I. "He's a friend of my pa's."

Willie didn't say nothin'.

Then I says, "Didn't you see a couple of men standin' on the back platform?"

"No," says Willie. "I can't be watchin' things like that when I'm takin' care of a switch and all that."

Mitch looked at me. We knew then it was all right. So I started in on the money.

"Look here, Willie, this here conductor hit us for two dollars, a dollar apiece for our fare to Havaner."

"No," says Willie.

"Honest, didn't he, Mitch?"

Mitch said, "Yep."

"Well, he must be foolin'," says Willie, "for the fare is only 60 cents from Atterberry, and you'd go half fare at 30 cents."

Mitch says, "I've heard about conductors knockin' down, and this looks like it to me. But what's two dollars? When we get to Havaner, Skeet's pa will give him that twice over, if he wants it. So let it go, Skeet. If a conductor wants to be mean enough to cheat a couple of boys, and the railroad is mean enough to take the money, I say, let it go."

We hadn't gone more'n six miles anyway when the train stopped again. Willie and the conductor went way up toward the engine, and we was stalled here for most an hour. It was a hot box or somethin'. And we got tired and we was as hungry as wolves, since we hadn't et anything since morning.

Pretty soon Willie came in and says, "She's whistlin' for Havaner." We curved around by a sand hill and drew up by the depot. The sun was just above the tree tops. It had taken us hours and hours to come from

Atterberry, and Willie said it wasn't more'n forty miles. We hopped off and started away.

"Here," said the conductor. "Here's the receipt for your fare." He slipped the two dollars into my hand with a laugh, and we shook hands with Willie Wallace and started up town.

CHAPTER XVIII

IT seemed sad to part with Willie Wallace at the depot, but things was changed. He wasn't rollickin' and free no more, but looked serious and busy. Havaner was a big town, so there was a lot of switchin' to do, and Willie just said, "Good luck, boys," and disappeared sommers between cars. Then we started up the street, goin' to the steamboat landin'.

It must have been more'n a mile; and the sun was goin' down now and we began to wonder about the night. By and by, after inquirin' several times, we found the street that went to the landin' and hurried down. Well, here was a river! How could the Mississippi be much bigger? It was twict as big as the Sangamon, or bigger, and the big sycamore trees on the other side looked a mile away. And here was a bridge way up in the air crossin' the river for wagons and people, and furder down a railroad bridge, and you could look up or down the river for miles. Says I to Mitch, "How do you like this?" Says he, "Wal, sir, I just feel as if I could fly, I am that happy." There was lots of house boats on the shore, where fishermen lived; there was nets stretched out on the sand; and some wound up on reels, and there was just sloughs of row boats, and a good many people movin' around, and some dogs barkin', and the sun was just gettin' behind the woods on the other side of the river.

So then we began to ask when there was a steamboat to St. Louis. And a man said, "To-night. Hey, Bill," he called to another feller, "ain't the *City of Peoria* goin' down to-night?" The feller called back "yes." Mitch's eyes just glowed. He just stepped aside and I did and he said, "Now luck is with us." Then I said, "Let's ask somebody else about the boat, we might as well be sure." Just then a big boy came along, about eighteen, so we asked him. He was carryin' some fish and was in a hurry, and he said, "No boat for a week, kids," and went right on. That took the spirit out of us. So we went to a house-boat and asked a woman who was cookin' supper and she said she didn't know whether the St. Louis boat was a day late or not; that sometimes it was a day late, and if it was, it wouldn't be in till day after to-morrow. Just then her husband came up and heard us, and he said, "'Pears to me the boat went down last night. I can't ricollect. We don't pay much attention to the boats, havin' our own business to watch. But," says the man, "if you go up to the hotel, they have a time card up there; or I'll tell you, go over there to the landing, and look on the door of the office, and see if there ain't a time card tacked up." So we hurried over there, but some one had torn off the card, and the office was closed. Then we went up to the hotel.

We could see into the dinin' room and see the waitress girls carryin' trays and the food smelt wonderful, but it was fifty cents to eat and we couldn't afford it. Anyway we came up to ask about the boat. There was a gray-haired little feller standin' behind the desk, and awful busy with people comin' and goin', and we stood there tryin' to get in a word; but just as one of us would say, "What time —" a man would step up and say:

"I'm checkin' out," or "Let me have 201 again," or
somethin' like that. Finally nobody was there and Mitch
got it out, "When does the steamboat go to St. Louis?"

The little feller didn't look at Mitch, he looked at
me stiddy a long while. Then he looked at Mitch and
back again at me. And he says: "Ain't you the son of
States Attorney Kirby?" He got me so quick I couldn't
say nothin', so I says, "Yes, sir." "Wal," says he, "I
thought so. You look like him. And I believe you boys
are runnin' away. I think I'll turn you over to the
policeman."

So I stood there and said to myself, "It's ended —
we're done." And I was so scared I couldn't move. And
just then Mitch began to talk, and he says: "You can't,
because we just talked to him ourselves, and asked him
about the boat, and he's gone home to supper, and he
knows us and knows where we're visitin' with my aunt
here in Havaner. And if you don't want to tell us when
the boat comes in so we can go down and look at her
and really see a steamboat, all right."

Just then the bus backed up to the hotel and a lot of
men got out with satchels and came hurryin' in and
writin' their names in the book and gettin' rooms and
things — and while the clerk was flustered with this
business, we sneaked out.

So then we was pretty hungry and we went back to
the river, I don't know just why. But we came to the
fisherman's boat again, where the woman was cookin'
supper, and said she, "Did you find out when the boat
comes?" And we said no, but we asked her if we could
have some fried fish for a nickel and she says "yes," and
asked us in, and so Mitch and me sat with the fambly
and looked out of the little winder at the river and et

all the cat fish we wanted, with corn bread and onions
and things. There was a baby at the table and his nose
kept runnin' and his ma just let it; and besides there
was a little girl with hands as little as a bird's and black

"AIN'T YOU THE SON OF STATES ATTORNEY KIRBY?"

eyes and a pig tail, which made her hair as tight around
her head as a drum; and besides them, two boys and a
man who boarded there and the husband. And we
could see the bed to one side and some cots. They all
lived here together, right on the river, with the mosquitoes and the flies, which was awful. And at supper the

man said : "Now ain't it funny that nobody can tell about the boat! She's comin' in to-night from St. Louis and will land about 11, like she allus does. And she goes back to-morrow, or the next day, I forget which. Sometimes she changes her schedule and don't go back till Saturday — and sometimes they get up an excursion here to go up to Copperas Creek, and then she don't

LOOKING STRAIGHT UP INTO THE SKY

go back until that's over. But when she gets in, just ask the captain, and he'll know for sure."

After supper, we walked out by the river. We waited till about eight o'clock and then took a swim, and I was beginnin' to think where we was goin' to sleep. But Mitch had decided that. There was a shed near the shore with the slant away from the river, and Mitch says, "That's the place. The water moccasins won't bother us there, and the mosquitoes won't, after a bit, and we

can see down the river for miles, and see the *City of
Peoria* when she first turns the bend down there." So
we got up on the shed and lay down lookin' straight up
into the sky at the stars. It was a clear night and as
quiet as a graveyard, only now and then we heard a
voice, or a dog bark, or the dip of an oar in the river.
And Mitch lay with his hands under his head lookin'
up at the stars and not sayin' anything. After a while
he says: "Skeet, I told you there was somethin' on my
mind, and there is. There's more than one thing on my
mind, but I'm just wonderin' whether I'll tell you all
of it or not."

"Why not?" says I.

"Because about one thing I don't know what I'm
goin' to do myself, and if I talk about it, I'm likely to say
I'll do this or that, and then if I don't you'll wonder;
and I believe until I know just what I'm goin' to do,
I'd better keep still. And as far as that goes, this goin'
to see Tom Sawyer might have something to do with it.
We might not come back — or get back in time for this
thing that's in my mind. Although it don't take long
to come back. And so, considerin' everything, I decided
I'd take a chance, for we must see Tom Sawyer, Skeet;
it must be and it has to be now. You see I'm a little
mixed up after all; and ain't grown folks mixed up?
I never see anybody more mixed about what to do than
my pa sometimes. But I'll tell you this much, Skeet,
we wouldn't be here to-night, and we wouldn't be on
our way now to see Tom Sawyer if it warn't for one
thing."

"What's that?" says I.

"Zueline," says Mitch. Then Mitch began to shake,
and I knew he was cryin', and he took his hands from

under his head and put them over his eyes, and everything was so still it scared me. Then Mitch quit shakin'
and took his hands off his eyes and looked straight up
and was still for a long while. I couldn't guess what
was the matter. Had Zueline died, maybe, or gone
visitin', or quarreled with Mitch? So after a bit I says:
"Well, Mitch, you know me — I'm true blue, and I'll
stand by you, and if you want to tell me, just tell me,
and I'll never peach as long as I live."

So Mitch says: "Well, Skeet, I have a different
feelin' toward you from what I have towards Zueline.
You see I don't want to protect you, or take care of
you, and of course I'd fight for you, or help you any
way I could. But it's different with Zueline — I'd
die for her, and sometimes I want to, specially if she'd
die at the same time, and our funerals could be together
and we could be buried in the same grave. I have the
same feelin' about her that I have when I look at them
stars, I just get full in the throat, and don't know what
I am or where I am, or what to do."

"Well," says I, "I know that, Mitch, leastways I
suspicioned it — or somethin' like it, from the way you
always treated Zueline, but tell me what in the world
has happened."

"The worst has happened," says Mitch. "They've
taken her away from me."

"How do you mean?" says I.

"Well," says Mitch, "the day before I came out to
the farm to get you, Mrs. Hasson came over to see
ma. I was out in the yard gettin' some kindlin' for the
wood box, and I saw Mrs. Hasson coming. She never
comes to see ma, and I wondered what it could be about.
So I went up-stairs and looked down into the settin'

room through the pipe-hole in the floor and heard everything they said. And this is about it.

"Mrs. Hasson began by sayin' to ma: 'I think you
have a very remarkable boy, and I don't want to see any
harm come to him, and so I've come over here, Mrs.
Miller, to talk about your boy and Zueline.' 'What's
the matter?' says ma, in a scared way. 'Nothing,' says
Mrs. Hasson, 'except I never see a boy of his age so at-
tached to a girl, so in love with her,' she says, 'for that's
it; and it won't do.' And ma says, 'I never noticed it.
Of course I knew they played ₁together and was little
sweethearts like children will be. All the children play
together just like lambs, as you might say.' 'Well,'
says Mrs. Hasson, 'they are lambs; Zueline is a lamb
and so is Mitch. But it's clear out of the way for children
to have such a deep feelin' for each other — it scares me.
And while I don't think Zueline feels exactly the same
way, it's not the thing for a girl of twelve to be so much
taken up with a little boy; nor for a little boy to be so
completely absorbed in a little girl. So I've come over
to tell you that we must work together to separate 'em;
and to begin with, I'm goin' to take Zueline away for a
visit, and that will help to break it, and by the time she
gets back, it will be over or nearly so; and if it ain't,
we must work together to keep them away from each
other. Zueline can't come here any more; and Mitchie
mustn't come to our house, and they mustn't go to par-
ties where they meet.' So ma said she thought so too."

Here Mitch grew still and he began to shake again,
and I just lay there and looked at the stars and waited.
Finally Mitch started again:

"Skeet, when I heard this, I grew cold all over —
my whole body got prickly, my brain began to tingle,

the sweat started out on my face, I was just as weak as a cat. I just rolled over on my back as if I was dead. It was just the same as if you said to a feller: 'you have just a minute to live.' I lay there and heard 'em talk about church and a lot of other things, and then I heard Mrs. Hasson say she had to go, and I heard her walk out, and down the walk, and I heard the gate click. She was gone. The thing was done. I had lost Zueline. And I'll never get over it. It don't make no difference if I live to be a thousand years old, I'll never get over it. I'll never love any one else; I'll never feel the same again. And when I went down-stairs and began to carry in the kindlin', ma came into the kitchen. And after a bit she said: 'Mitchie, I want you to do a lot in school this fall and winter. I want you to put your mind on it, for I think you're goin' to be a man in the world and I want you to get ready. And you mustn't waste so much time on Zueline. She's just a little girl and you're just a little boy; and she seems awful pretty to you now, but she ain't really pretty. She won't be a pretty woman. I can see that now, but you can't. She's goin' to have more or less of a hard face like her mother. And if she was the girl for you, and I could see it, I wouldn't say this. But I know she isn't. She won't be good enough for you. And, besides, this boy and girl business is all foolishness and you must stop it. I've already told Mrs. Hasson that I think it ought to be stopped.' Do you see how good ma was? She wanted me to think it was her and not Mrs. Hasson that was interferin'. But I was cold all through, and turned to stone like. My eyes felt hard and tight like buttons, and I laughed — Yep, I really laughed, and said to ma — 'All right, ma. I'll obey you.' And she says: 'You're a good boy, and I

love you most to death.' So then I couldn't sleep that
night, and the next mornin' I started early for the farm,
to get you to go now to see Tom Sawyer; for when a
thing like this happens, the only thing to do is to go away,
just as fur as you can."

Mitch had been talkin' slower and slower, and finally
he gave a kind of long breath, and I knew he was asleep.
I crawled to the edge of the roof and looked out at the
river, at the red lanterns on the bridge which was re-
flected in the water, at the river, which I could see movin'
like a tired snake, at the dark woods across the river.
Then I slid back near to Mitch and fell asleep too.

CHAPTER XIX

SOMETHING woke me up. I don't know what. I didn't know where I was at first. There wasn't a sound except a dog barkin' way off. Mitch was sound asleep. Pretty soon I thought I heard somethin' way down the river. I kept lookin', past the bridge where the red lanterns hung, way down into the darkness of the river, between the woods. And all of a sudden I saw two lights, then more lights, then fire shot straight up from smokestacks. It was a steamboat. It must be the *City of Peoria*, from St. Louis.

I shook Mitch and got him to. He rubbed his eyes, then jumped up sudden and strong. He stood up and looked. "Skeet," he says, "there she is. Who knows Tom Sawyer may have seen her this week or last week? Tom Sawyer may have been on her. What would you think if Tom Sawyer was actually on her, takin' a trip? For he can go anywheres he wants to, havin' as much money as he has."

So we stood up and watched her. And pretty soon we could hear her puff, and see all the lights and see the fire and the sparks shoot out of the smokestacks; and as far as I could see, there wasn't no one but Mitch and me watchin' her and waitin' for her to come in. It se_ she'd never get in. She puffed and blowed. Th_ must have been awful strong. By and _ we could hear voices on her; we _

And finally she came under the bridge, blowin' smoke and noise right against the floor of the bridge with a louder noise. That was about a half a mile away, it seemed. And pretty soon then she swung to right opposite the shed where we was, and nosed in. They threw down a gang plank and the men began to work, niggers and such. We went down and watched 'em. The captain came along, and Mitch says to me, " Now we got to find out about the boat, and we've got to get a job on her and work our way. We must hang on to our money as long as we can." So Mitch went right up to the captain and says : "Can we get a job on this here boat, me and my chum?"

The captain says, "What can you do?"

"We can do anything," says Mitch.

"Can you peel potatoes, and carry water, and wait on table?"

"Yes, sir," says Mitch.

"All right," says the captain. "You're hired; ten cents a day and board. Report in the mornin' at six o'clock."

"I'm ready now," says Mitch.

"Report in the mornin'," says the captain.

Then Mitch says : "Why can't we go on board now, and go to bed and be ready when six o'clock comes?"

Just then he began to holler at some niggers carryin' some boxes, and he said to us, "Get out of the way there." We stepped aside, and the niggers got between us and the captain, and when they was past the captain had disappeared. We couldn't see him nowheres. There was a man standin' there, a kind of boss, it seemed. So we asked him when the boat was goin' back to St. Louis, and he said to-morrow at noon. Then another boss spoke up and said, "No, we're goin' up to Copperas Creek, back Saturday." "Who says so?" "Well, that's the talk." "You didn't get that from the captain." "No, but that's the talk."

"Gee," said Mitch, "what wouldn't you give to sleep on her? We could sleep on the deck. Let's wait and ask the captain."

We waited around for about an hour. But the captain didn't appear. Then Mitch says: "Come on, Skeet, we're hired, we belong on this boat, we have a right to get on her, let's climb around there up to the deck."

So we watched so nobody could see us. We climbed around, up the poles, over the railing, and got on to the deck. It was way off toward the bow and nobody was there. We looked at the river a bit. Things got quieter

SUSIE SKINNER

and quieter. Finally we lay down on the deck and fell asleep.

And pretty soon I began to feel it was gettin' daylight. I didn't sleep very well. And by and by I felt somebody nudgin' me, and I opened my eyes, and there stood a man in a white apron with a white cap on. And he says, "Here, what you doin' here? You ain't got no right on this boat." He nudged Mitch, and Mitch woke up. Then the man said, "Where do you boys belong? Did you get on at Bath, or Beardstown?"

"We got on here," says Mitch. "We're hired. The captain hired us to peel potatoes and carry water, and we're here ready to work."

"You are, are you?" says the cook, for it was the cook. "Well, then, come along. It's half past five, and time to go to work."

He took us to the kitchen and set us to work. First we both peeled potatoes. Then he set us doin' all sorts of things, carryin' dishes, bringin' his terbaker, and I had to carry water; and finally he made me wipe dishes which a girl was washin'. And such a lot of swearin' you never heard in your life. The cook was singin' a song which went somethin' like this, as far as I can remember:

> There was a little girl, and she lived with her mother,
> And the world all over couldn't find such a nother,
> Tum-a-ter-a-um-a lida bugaroo,
> Tum-a-ter-a-um-a lida bugaroo.
>
> She had hair on her head like thorns on the hedges,
> And the teeth in her jaws was a set of iron wedges,
> Tum-a-ter-a-um-a lida bugaroo,
> Tum-a-ter-a-um-a lida bugaroo.

And he was throwin' things into the skillet and callin' to the girl who was washin' dishes. She wore slippers that slipped back and forth on her feet; her apron was twisted; her hair was twisted in a little knot; she had on a brass ring, and he called her Susie. Then he'd sing:

> There goes Susie Skinner,
> How in the hell you know?
> I know her by her apron strings,
> And her shoe strings draggin' on the floor,
> Gol dern her,
> And her shoe strings draggin' on the floor.

By and by breakfast was ready, and Mitch and me could hardly wait. We couldn't eat till all the passengers was served, for they made us go in and take away the soiled dishes. And so when it came our turn, we just pitched into the liver and potatoes and the pancakes.

And it must have been about half past ten, and hot. It was hot like the sun under a burning glass, and the river smelled and the dead fish. Only a little breeze began to stir after a while, and then it was better. We had nothin' to do now, and stood by the railin' lookin' at the kids on shore. "Don't you bet they wish they were here?" said Mitch. "Well, we've struck it, at last, and by Saturday, we'll see Tom Sawyer, and tell him all about our trip."

I began to hear the sound of a fiddle, and a lot of laughin'; so Mitch and me edged around the deck till we got toward the front right under the little cupola where the wheel was, where the captain stood when the boat was runnin'. And there sat a lot of men, the captain and several others, with some glasses and beer bottles; and a white-haired man, his name was Col. Lambkin, with his mustache curled and waxed up and all white too, was dancin' as nimble as a boy. This fiddler was playin' somethin' awful devilish and quick, and the rest was pattin' their hands and feet while the old feller was dancin'. He was dressed in a fine, tight fittin' coat and had on varnished shoes, and a panama hat with a string buttoned into his lapel so his hat wouldn't blow away; and a diamond in his necktie, and one on his hand that I could see glitter as he danced.

We got up closer, and the captain saw us and said: "Come over here now and do a jig — come on."

The fiddler stopped playin' and looked around. It

was John Armstrong. First he looked at me, then he looked down at the floor, kind a funny like, and then he raised his eyes and looked at us again. We just stood there, not knowin' what to do. Then John said: "Wal, boys, when did you come?"

The captain said, "Do you know them kids, John?" John says: "Come over here, boys, and I'll introduce

AND THERE SAT A LOT OF MEN

you to the captain." We walked over. John said: "This here is preacher Miller's boy over at Petersburg. And this here is the son of States Attorney Kirby. You know Hardy Kirby." The captain said "yes." John went on, "Of course you do." And then the captain says: "I hired 'em to peel potatoes; they're goin' to St. Louis with me." "Is that so?" said John. "Well, they're good boys, and of course you'll fotch 'em back when you get through with 'em." "I don't know," says the captain, "I may sell 'em in St. Louis — or adopt 'em. I ain't got no boys of my own, and if they prove all right, good workers, I may keep 'em for good." John laughed. Kept laughin' at everything that was said. And finally they drank more beer and all talked together; and the old feller that was dancin' sat down, lit a fine cigar, and began to tell about New York. It turned out he was the fish commissioner and lived in Havaner; but he had traveled everywhere and was a regular gentleman. And finally he says to the captain — "Sing the 'Missouri Harmony.'" "I will," says the captain, "if John'll play the tune." So John played it and the captain sang.

I forgot to say that I can't remember nothin', or commit anything to memory. But I never see such a boy as Mitch. He could learn anything, and that's how I happen to write these songs down here. He wrote 'em out for me afterwards and handed 'em to me. Well, this is what the captain sang:

> When in death I shall calm recline,
> O bear my heart to my mistress dear.
>
> Tell her it lived on smiles and wine
> Of brightest hue while it languished here.
>
> Bid her not shed one tear of sorrow,
> To sully a heart so brilliant and light,
>
> But balmy drops of the red grape borrow
> To bathe the relict from morn till night.

He sang it in kind of a sing song. Then John kept tellin' stories and fiddlin'; and finally he struck up a tune that was more lively than any, and the white-haired gentleman got up and danced faster and gracefuler than ever. Then John told a story. Everybody was laughin'. By this time the captain had Mitch on his knee, and you never did see such fun and good friendship; and a man who'd been keepin' quiet except for laughin' pulled me over to him and said, "You look like your dad. Your dad is the best man in this county, the best lawyer and the best friend. You be as good as your dad, and you're all right." I said, "Yes, sir," and was almost too happy to live.

Then the party kind a broke up. The old gentleman was talkin' to a fat man, who was pretty full of beer; and John was talkin' to the captain. Mitch and me just sat there and watched. Then I heard John ask the captain, "When you goin' to pull out?" "Not till Saturday," said the captain. "To-morrow or next day we may pull up to Copperas Creek; but we won't go back till Saturday." "Wal," says John, "is that so? Not till a Saturday?"

Mitch and me thought it was time to start to help with the dinner. So we went away and the party seemed to break up. We got the potatoes peeled and finally everything was cooked and all ready, and we was about to help wait on the table as before, when one of the waiters came in and said, "The captain wants to see you, boys." So we went in and there was the captain at his own table with John and Col. Lambkin, and all the rest of the men just ready to eat. And the captain says, "Here, boys, come and sit here with us." So then we were at the captain's table, with the waiters waitin' on us and lookin' kind of funny to see what had happened and wonderin' why.

And at the dinner table John says: "Why don't you boys come home with me, and then come back here a Saturday, and catch the boat? You must visit me some time and why not now? There never was a better time."

The captain says: "That's the thing to do, boys. We're goin' up to Copperas Creek and there ain't a thing in that. And you can go over and have your visit, and John will bring you back. Your job will be waitin' for you, and I promise you I'll take you to St. Louis and back to Havaner."

"No," said Mitch, "we'll stick to our jobs." Then the captain says, "You're fired till Saturday. I won't have you around till Saturday. There's goin' to be an Odd Fellows' Excursion, and it's no place for boys, and so you can make the best of it."

Then John said, "That's the thing to do, boys. I'll play the fiddle for you; Aunt Caroline will be glad to see you, and we'll have a good time."

Mitch looked disappointed, but there we were. We couldn't stay on the boat, there was nothin' to do in Havaner, so we gave up.

And by and by we left the boat, saying good-by to the captain, and went with John over into town, and down to the court house to get his team to go home.

CHAPTER XX

JOHN went to the rack to untie his horses and Mitch and me was standin' off waitin' to get in the wagon. Mitch said in kind of a low voice, "This don't seem right to me. I've got a kind of feelin' we'll not come back; that we'll miss the boat or somethin'. I feel a little as if we're being tricked."

I said, "No, Mitch, how can it be? You don't think John Armstrong came on purpose to the boat to catch us, do you?"

"No," said Mitch.

"He couldn't know we're on the boat. Well, then, where's the trick?"

Said Mitch, "Well, he knows our pas, he knows we'd started for St. Louis, and maybe just as a good turn to our pas, he fixed it with the captain to get us off the boat and bring us to his house."

Says I, "That can't be, Mitch. In the first place, he's wanted us to visit him for a long while, and in the next place, what'd be the use of him interferin' this way and takin' us to his house? He knows we could steal out of the window to-night, or walk away to-morrow mornin'. It ain't only six miles from his house to Havaner, and we can be back here by Saturday in spite of anything."

Mitch says, "Yes, but suppose he telegraphs or somethin' to our folks, and they come and get us."

"Well," says I, "if we see any sign of that, we'll sneak. Besides, John don't know enough to telegraph.

He never telegraphed in his life. And the mail is too slow. I tell you what let's do, let's stay with John to-night and to-morrow after dinner wander off and come back here."

"That's it," said Mitch. "That is what we'll do. But anyway you take it the jig's up if they want it to be. Because they could catch us on the boat if they wanted to. John knows we're goin' on the boat, and if he peaches, why, we're caught."

John backed up the horses and we got in and so started off. Then Mitch began to feel John out. As we passed the depot he says: "I suppose you don't want to telegraph Aunt Caroline (that was John's wife) that we're comin' and you've got company."

"Telegraph," says John, with a chuckle and a giggle. "Why, I never sent a telegram in my life, and besides Aunt Caroline always has enough to eat, and we have two spare beds, so what's the use of wastin' money on a telegram?"

I nudged Mitch. A part of the way to John's we went along the edge of a place where nothin' growed at all. There wasn't a weed or a tree. John said it was the Mason County desert, and onct he got over in there and got lost, that there wasn't a livin' thing in there, and not a crow ever flew over it.

And then we came to Oakford — not as nice a town as Bobtown, the houses not so white, and not the same well-kept look. But John had a fine house, not very big, nice and comfortable with a big yard, and a brick walk and flowers. It was right at the edge of town and his farm went way off clear to the woods.

Aunt Caroline just said howdy and smiled and went into the kitchen; and John went to the sink and washed

out of a pan and we did, and then we had supper; the
most jellies I ever saw, and wild honey, and cold ham,
and fried chicken, and several kinds of bread, and cake
and berries and cream. So after that Mitch and me
was about caught up on meals. John talked all the time
at supper and swore a good deal, about every other
word, not the worst swearin', but regular swearin';
and he kept tellin' one thing and then another about
folks around the country, things that had happened.
But all the time Aunt Caroline just set there and et and
never said a word.

After supper John said he'd go over and get Vangy
to play the organ and keep time for him. Says he,
"You can't fiddle without a organ or somethin' to keep
time. That warn't no fiddlin' on the boat." So John
went out and that left us with Aunt Caroline, and she
just cleaned up the dishes awful nice and orderly, but
never said nothin' — not a word.

John was gone at least half an hour. He came in
then and said Vangy would be over, then he went to a
trunk and got out a Bible, and showed it to us. And
says he, "Linkern read out of this, by God." That was
the swear word he kept usin', and I don't like to use it,
and won't again. But when I say John swore, you'll
know what I mean. "Yes, sir (swear word), this is the
Bible. It belongs (swear word) to old Aunt Sarie Rutledge (swear word), and I borrowed it off'n her to show
your pa one time and never hain't took it back. Aunt
Sarie is a relative of Jasper, the Sheriff (swear word)."
So he put that back. Then he showed us a picture of
Duff, his brother, which Linkern defended for murder,
and a picture of one of the jurymen what let Duff off,
and a picture of his mother's brother what was the

greatest fiddler ever in the county. And he showed us
Duff's discharge from the army which Linkern wrote,
and a badge which Linkern had given to his mother
onct. So then I said to John, "Did you ever see Mr.
Linkern?"

Said John, "Lots of times (swear word). I heard him
make a speech over at Havaner against Douglas. Douglas warn't there, but it were agin him (swear word)."

Then Mitch said, "How did he look?" "Wal (swear
word)," says John, "he was just sottin' on the platform
and he looked like he didn't have no sense, kind a dull;
and his legs was so long that his jints stuck up above his
ears like a grasshopper with his jints above his back.
But when he got up to talk, he changed. His face got
lively like, and he took everybody right off their feet."

So I, bein' the States Attorney's son, was interested
in Duff's case, and I asked John if he heard the trial.

"No, sir," said John, "I didn't. I had the ager and
couldn't go. You see he warn't tried at Havaner, but
down at Beardstown, and the only time I went thar was
when I went to see Duff with my mother, while Duff
was thar in jail."

"Did you see him?" asked Mitch. "Yes (swear
word)," said John, "he was thar. He was sottin' thar,
him and another feller. Thar they was in jail. And I
said to Duff, 'What's he in thar fur?' Said Duff: 'Stole
one of them Shanghai roosters (swear word) wuth five
dollars; stand on thar feet and pick corn off'n a table
like that.'"

"How long was Duff in jail?" asked Mitch.

"Well, sir (swear word) he must have been thar most
of the fall. I don't recollect; and then they had the
trial and Linkern cleared him with a almanac."

"How's that?" says I.

"Wal (swear word), they was witnesses that swore they seed Duff hit this feller with a sling-shot, and they seed it because the moon was bright right at the meridian. And Linkern got every witness to go over it again and say the moon was at the meridian, and that's why they seed Duff hit this feller with a sling-shot; and after Linkern had got it all clear by cross questionin' these witnesses, then he pulled out a almanac, and says to the judge and the jury, 'Look here.' They looked and saw that the moon warn't at the meridian, but was a settin' (swear word); and so they couldn't have seed Duff hit him with a slung-shot. And Linkern put a feller on the stand and axed him 'Did you ever make a slung-shot?' 'Yes,' says he. 'Tell me how,' says Linkern. 'Wal,' says he, 'I took a egg shell and sunk one half of it in the sand; then I melted some zinc and lead and poured it into the egg shell, and made two of these; then I took a old boot and cut out some leather and sewed the leather around these two halves with squirrel's hide; then I made a loop for the wrist of squirrel's hide'; and then Linkern says, 'Look at this.' He handed a slung-shot to the feller; and says, 'Take your knife and rip it open.' So he did, and there fell out the two halves molded in this here egg shell, and so the slung-shot belonged to this feller and didn't belong to Duff at all. And they had found it thar where the fight was; but every one fit that night (swear word). You see they were a-holdin' a camp meetin', and about a mile off thar was a bar where they sold drinks, and they'd go and get religion a little (swear word), and then go and get some drinks, and so on back and forth, and so they fit. And this here feller that was killed and Duff fit here onct right in Oakford, because he pulled Duff off'n a barl where he was sleepin', and Duff got up and whooped him."

By this time Vangy came in. And Mitch was in the best of spirits. I never heard him laugh so much.

Vangy sat down to the organ, and John tuned up his fiddle, and they started. Aunt Caroline came in then and sot down and began to knit, but didn't say nothin'. John just drew a few times with his bow and then he said: "This here is called 'Pete McCue's Straw Stack,' named after old Peter McCue who lived down by Tar Creek. They had a dance thar and the fellers hitched their horses clost to a straw stack in the lot and when they came out the horses had et all the straw stack up. So they had been a playin' this here tune and after that they called it 'Pete McCue's Straw Stack.'"

Then John played it, tappin' his foot, and Vangy just made the organ talk. She was as thin as a killdeer, and looked consumptive, but she knew how to play the organ, you bet.

Then John began to laugh and he says, "Thar was a feller over near Salt Creek named Clay Bailey, that tried to play the fiddle, but he never played but one tune, and they called it 'Chaw Roast Beef.' He warn't a very big man, but round chested and stout, and he came here onct when Porky Jim Thomas was runnin' a saloon here, before he moved to Bobtown. Wal, this here Clay Bailey was in thar havin' some drinks with the boys, and all at onct a feller came in with his coat tail all chawed off, and lookin' pretty blue and he said a bull dog had come fur him. Clay would fight anything. And so he says to the stranger, 'You buy the drinks, and I'll go out and whoop the bull.' 'All right,' says the stranger. So he bought the drinks and Clay went out, follered

by the hull crowd. The bull belonged to one of the Watkinses and was in a wagon watchin'; so Clay went
right up to the wagon and the bull jumped for him.
Clay caught him by the ear and held him off with one
hand and pounded him over the heart with his fist, till
the bull gave up. Then Clay flung him down like, and

JOHN ARMSTRONG PLAYS THE FIDDLE

the bull got up and run about 40 rods down to a walnut
tree and stood there and just bellered as if the moon
was shinin'. Now, Vangy, 'Chaw Roast Beef.'"

So John played that and Mitch was rollin' from side
to side in his chair and laughin' fit to kill. Then John
said, "I s'pose you boys never seed no platform dancin'."

M

We never had and wanted to know what it was. "Wal (swear word)," says John, "they put up a platform and one after another they get up on the platform and dance, and when they get real earnest they take their shoes off. Jim Tate who went out to Kansas was the best platform dancer we ever had around here. He came over one night to Old Uncle Billy Bralin's whar my uncle was a fiddlin' — the best fiddler they ever was here. And Jim heard him and got to jigglin' and finally he looked in the room and he says, 'Clar the cheers out, I'm goin' to take off my shoes and come down on her.' So they did, and while he was dancin' his foot went through one of the holes in the puncheon floor and skinned one of his shins. Up to then they had always called this piece 'Shoats in the Corn,' but after that they called it 'Skinnin' your Shins.' Go ahead, Vangy." Then he played "Skinnin' your Shins," and after that "Rocky Road to Jordan," "Way up to Tar Creek," "A Sly Wink at Me," "All a Time a Goin' with the High Toned Gals," and a lot more that I can't remember, and between every piece he'd tell a story.

Then John began to get tired, and it was about ten o'clock. So Vangy went home, and we all went to bed. And after Mitch and me got in bed, I heard him laughin' to himself, and I says, "What's the matter, Mitch?" And he says, "This is the funniest thing I ever see, I wouldn't have missed this for anything." Then we fell asleep.

The next mornin' Aunt Caroline had the wonderfulest breakfast you ever saw: waffles, honey, bacon, eggs, and John just et and talked and kept swearin'. And Aunt Caroline sat lookin' down at her plate eatin' and didn't say nothin' — just looked calm and happy.

John seemed to have some kind of business that mornin'. Anyway he went away for a bit and left us to ourselves lookin' about the place and goin' over some photographs Aunt Caroline had. By and by Vangy came in and John. And John got out the fiddle again, to play a piece he called "Injun Puddin'" and so the fun was startin' all over again. There was a knock at the door and Aunt Caroline went and opened it, and there stood my pa and Mr. Miller. "Well, you young pirates," said my pa, as he came in the room, "you're goin' down to see Tom Sawyer, are you, and run away from your home?"

"They got a job on the steamboat, Hard," said John. "You can't interfere with that, you know." And he laughed and swore.

"I'll get a switch to you, young man," my pa went on. "Mitchie, what makes you do this?" asked Mr. Miller. "It does beat the world. Your mother is worried almost to death."

Mitch looked down. I was still because I was scared. Pretty soon everything got jolly again. John fiddled some more. They all told stories, the funniest you ever heard, and everybody laughed. I saw Aunt Caroline smile clear across her face. Then we had a grand dinner. And when the train came in, my pa and Mr. Miller put us on and took us back to Petersburg.

Of course John Armstrong tricked us, but when did he do it — and how? I don't know.

CHAPTER XXI

EVERYTHING seemed changed now. My ma wasn't the same, the house wasn't the same; Myrtle was talkin' about girls and boys I didn't know. Maud Fisher had come back from Chicago where she had visited and Myrtle was goin' up the hill to see her. Maud lived in a great brick house that looked like a castle. Her pa was one of the richest men in town and they lived splendid.

And Mitch was changed too. We hadn't found the treasure; we had been cheated out of our trip to St. Louis, for they wouldn't let us go back to Hanaver to get the boat; we hadn't seen Tom Sawyer. And Mr. Miller had told Mitch a lot of stories of Shakespeare and had set him to readin', and Mitch had read a lot of it, and told me about Hamlet who lost his father, and killed his step-father, and saw his mother drink poison; and had lost his girl too, and lost everything. And Mitch says, "Pa says that is about the way. This life is sorrow, you always lose, you never win, and if you do, it's worse'n if you lost; and you're just bein' put through a kind of schoolin' for somethin' else. For if you have trouble, then you are made wise and kind, maybe, or at least you can be; and so there's something after this life where you can use your mind as it has been made better by this life."

Well, you see, I couldn't believe this. How about John Armstrong and Col. Lambkin, and the captain?

Warn't they happy? Wasn't my grandma happy and my grandpa? There must be a way. Some folks must have luck, even if others don't; so I did my best to cheer Mitch up.

But now we was separated a good deal. For to watch me, pa took me to his office where I had to sit all day mostly, and tell where he was, if I knew; and run errands, go over to the clerk's office for papers. And just now there was a good deal to do for court was comin' on, and they were getting ready to try Temple Scott for killin' Joe Rainey.

At last the judge came. He came right in to see my pa. He lived way off in Jerseyville in a different county. I don't believe Mitch and me was ever any gladder to see each other than pa and the judge. They talked politics and cases and about makin' speeches to juries; and they agreed that when you get up to talk you don't know what you are goin' to say, but you get started and you know when you get the swing, and are really cuttin' ice. So the judge was invited to our house for dinner, and ma bought a new lamp for the center table on account of it; and Myrtle was all dressed up, and so was I. And ma put on a lot of airs, stretchin' things a lot about her folks and her do'n's in society and pa's wonderful speeches — some the judge hadn't heard. And pa told some stories that I had heard him tell before; and when the judge spoke, every one was quiet and scared like, even pa seemed a little embarrassed. The judge asked me if I was goin' to be a lawyer, and I said no, a steamboat captain. Then they all laughed and pa said: "There's a story about that that I'll tell you, judge." Then I blushed and Myrtle giggled and ma looked mad, because she was really ashamed of me.

And finally the court opened. I went up to see what it was like. There sat the judge on a high seat. And different lawyers would get up and say, "Docket number 8020" or somethin'. And the judge would turn over the leaves of a book and say, "Kelly *vs.* Graves," or somethin' and wait. Then the lawyer would say, "Default of Nora Kennedy" or somethin'. Then the judge would write, and so on. And my pa acted as if he didn't know the judge at all. He always said "your honor," and the judge didn't call him Hardy like he did at our house, but always Mr. Kirby. Nobody could tell they knew each other.

The town was chuck full of people. Watermelon rinds was all over the court house yard and there was lots of fights and men gettin' drunk; and after a few days, the court room was full of people watchin' the court proceedings. It was lots better than a theater, though not so good as a circus. I got hold of Mitch finally and he came and sat with me. He got interested after a while, and whatever he got interested in, he watched and liked better than anybody. But one day when we was there my pa got up and told the judge he was ready to try Temple Scott for killin' Joe Rainey. Then a little man, wearin' nose glasses, awful cunnin' lookin', with a soft voice, which he could make deep when he wanted to, said he was ready. He was Major Abbott, Temple Scott's lawyer. And so the case started.

It went on several days with lots of witnesses testifyin' — all the people who practiced "Pinafore" that night told about hearing the shots. And this little lawyer whose name was Major Abbott, as I said, asked every one, "How many shots did you hear?" Most of 'em said two; but some said they couldn't remember; and he made some of 'em say they heard three shots. They had found two bullets in Joe Rainey, and the point seemed to be that the other shot was fired by Joe Rainey; for pa said to me one day when we was walkin' home at noon that the defense was that Joe Rainey fired at Temple Scott first.

Then Major Abbott cross-questioned the witnesses about whether they saw Joe Rainey come into the house and go out just before he was killed. And most of 'em said yes. And then he tried to get 'em to say that they saw Joe Rainey go up-stairs and come down and go out; but none of 'em would say this. Then he'd ask 'em if they didn't hear Joe Rainey say, "Where's my pistol?" speakin' to his wife; and if she didn't say, "You can't have it," and take hold of him, and if he didn't pull away from her and go up-stairs and come down; and then if they didn't hear a shot as if it was fired from the porch followed by two

MAJOR ABBOTT

shots. But he couldn't get the witnesses to say this, though he asked a lot of questions and worried 'em and tangled 'em about different things. And once in a while my pa would say, "I object, your honor." And the judge would say mostly "sustained," and Major Abbott would say, "Your honor will allow me an exception." "Let it be noted," said the judge, and so on.

All the time Mitch kept twistin' in his seat and sayin', "He's tryin' to get 'em to lie. That's what he's doin'."

Mrs. Rainey was in the court, sittin' behind the railing. Temple Scott sat behind Major Abbott at the trial table. My pa was on the other side, and Sheriff

MRS. RAINEY IN COURT

Rutledge kept runnin' in and out, bringin' in witnesses. They had Temple Scott's pistol there with two chambers empty, and the bullets which had been taken out of Joe Rainey's body, the same size as in Temple Scott's pistol. And they had a statement which Joe Rainey had made just before he died in which he swore that he didn't have no pistol, that he came just inside the door, thinkin' he would go to bed and leave Temple Scott, and then he came right out in order to quiet him and tell him he didn't mean anything and was his friend.

"That's the truth," says Mitch, "and I'll bet on it." This statement of Joe Rainey said that they had been playing cards and was friendly till they got out on the street, when he asked Scott not to come around his house any more, that he liked him and could be friends with him, but he didn't want him to visit any more with Mrs. Rainey. Mitch says: "I heard pa and ma talk about this and they said Temple Scott wanted to marry Mrs. Rainey." Well, that seemed to kind of get in the case without anybody testifyin' to it, exactly. The court room seemed to breathe that idea, and on the streets it was talked.

Finally Major Abbott stated his side of the case, and he put Mrs. Rainey on the witness stand, and she said Joe Rainey had come in the house and asked for his pistol, that she took hold of him and said, "You mustn't get your pistol," that he tore away from her and went up-stairs; and came runnin' down, that he went out, that she heard a shot, and then later two shots of a different sound, that they all rushed to the door and found Joe Rainey lyin' on the porch floor bleedin' and unconscious.

And my pa cross-questioned her and she rared up and said that Joe Rainey had brought Temple Scott to her house in the first place and introduced him and wanted him to come, and had him to meals, and that this talk of her carin' for Temple Scott was a base slander and the work of mean enemies. And that no gentleman would hint of such a thing. And as far as her testifyin' at all in the case, she wanted to see justice done, and to do it she went through this disagreeable experience, which was enough to kill anybody. Finally

ON THE STREET IT WAS TALKED

pa asked: "Where is Joe Rainey's pistol?" And she got mad and said, "I don't know where it is — nobody knows."

"Nobody knows," my pa asked quiet like.

"Nobody that I know of," she answered.

"Oh," said my pa.

Then Major Abbott sneered: "You got what you didn't want then." And the judge said: "Gentlemen, you must be courteous to each other. There has been entirely too much personalities in this case and it must stop."

Major Abbott got up to argue. The judge says: "There's nothing before the court, Major Abbott. Proceed with the case."

And Major Abbott said again: "Your honor will allow me an exception."

"Let it be noted," said the judge, and so on.

Other witnesses testified for Temple Scott and it all came to the same thing. There was three shots, and some testified that Joe Rainey had threatened Temple Scott. So pa made these witnesses or most of 'em say that they had been threatened too by Joe Rainey, and didn't believe he meant it, and that they warn't afraid of him. Finally Major Abbott got up and said: "We had a witness who saw Joe Rainey's pistol lying by the side of the porch, where it had evidently fallen out of his hand. But he has disappeared and we can't find where he is. With that out of the case, the defense rests."

Mitch began to get more and more nervous and to kind of talk to himself.

Then the judge asked, "Major Abbott, did you subpoena this witness?"

"No," said Major Abbott. "We should have done so, I confess, and I intended to. But I talked to him, he seemed entirely willing to testify; nevertheless I intended to subpoena him the first of the month and got ready to do so, and found that he had disappeared."

"What's his name?" said my pa real quick.

"His name," said Major Abbott in a deep voice and very calm, "is Harold Carman." That was the man who was takin' the part of one of the sailors in "Pinafore"; and sure enough he had disappeared and no one knew where.

So Major Abbott sat down in a satisfied way. Mitch says, "Why don't Temple Scott go on and tell that Joe Rainey shot at him?" "He don't have to," says I; "pa says no man has to testify against hisself, and you can't criticize him for it."

"Against hisself," said Mitch. "Why if he, Joe Rainey, shot at him first, he'd be testifyin' for hisself, and not against hisself. He darn't testify," says Mitch. "It's a lie. Joe Rainey didn't shoot at him. I can just see right through this case."

I believed Mitch, for besides everything else, he was the smartest boy I ever knew.

Then the judge asked pa — "Any rebuttal?" And pa says, "Just a few things, your honor, but it's now ten minutes to twelve, and near adjournin' time, and if your honor will indulge me, I'd like to have court adjourn now till one o'clock."

So the court said very well, and Sheriff Rutledge adjourned the court, and all the people began to go out.

And then I see for the first time that mornin' that Mr. Miller was in the court room. He rose up as my pa came down the aisle and spoke to him, and they walked away together and up the hill, goin' home together with Mitch and me follerin'. When we got to our house pa says, "I'm goin' up to Mr. Miller's for dinner, you tell your ma." And they all went away together, Mr. Miller, my pa, and Mitch.

CHAPTER XXII

I GOT back to the court room about ten minutes to one and only a few was there. It was awful interestin' now, and I couldn't keep away or hardly wait for the next thing. Pretty soon Mitch came in and set by me. His hair was combed slick, and he acted terribly quiet. Then the judge came and my pa and court was opened. Pretty soon Mr. Miller came in and sat with Mitch and me and after a while Mrs. Miller, who hadn't been there before, and my ma was with her. The court room was so full you couldn't breathe.

Then my pa got up and began to talk and he said he had some evidence which was competent, but needed to be explained first to the judge, and he thought they'd better go into the judge's room and talk about it first. So the judge, my pa, and Major Abbott went to the judge's room and closed the door, and the jury just waited and the audience began to whisper and I looked across the room and saw John Armstrong. Everybody was there except grandpa and grandma, Willie Wallace, my uncle and maybe a few others.

After a while the judge, my pa and Major Abbott came out of the judge's room. The judge got on the bench and said, "You may proceed, Mr. States Attorney."

My pa turned around and looked down in the audience, and said in a loud voice, "Mitchell Miller, take the witness stand, please."

I was knocked over. Here was Tom Sawyer right over again. Mitch was goin' to testify. What on earth did he know? He'd never told me a word.

Mitch was dreadful pale, and so was Mr. Miller. But Mr. Miller says, "Come on, my boy, and may God help you."

So they got up, and Mr. Miller walked with Mitch inside the railin' and stood there, very sad, until Mitch took the witness chair, then he walked back and sat down inside the railing.

All the jury was craning their necks now and the court room was so still that the tickin' of the clock was scary.

It seemed as Mitch was only twelve, they had to ask him about whether he knew what he was doin'. So my pa began this a way, after Mitch was sworn.

"What is your name?"

"Mitchell Miller."

"How old are you?"

"Twelve years old."

"Do you understand the obligations of an oath?"

"I do, sir."

"What are they?"

"They are to tell the truth, the whole truth, and nothing but the truth."

"And if you don't tell the truth, what will happen to you?"

"I'll be punished."

"How?"

"By prison."

"What else?"

"By God."

"You believe in God, do you, Mitchie?" asked my pa in a quieter voice.

"I do," said Mitch.

"And a hereafter."

"I do."

"And that you'll be punished in the hereafter if you don't tell the truth?"

"That's leading, your honor," interrupted Major Abbott.

"Yes," said the judge.

"Very well," said my pa.

"What else will happen to you if you don't tell the truth, Mitchell?"

"I'll be punished in the hereafter."

"Cross-examine," said my pa.

Then Major Abbott began in kind of a sneerin' voice. "So you think you'll be punished in the hereafter?"

"Yes, sir."

"Why?"

"Why wouldn't I be for swearin' a man's life away?"

"For swearin' a man's life away," repeated Major Abbott, kind of stunned.

"That's what I'm obliged to do," said Mitch.

"Well, one thing at a time, my boy," said the Major, a little friendlier. "Tell me now who told you about the obligations of an oath."

"I've read about it," said Mitch.

"Where?"

"In Blackstone's Commentaries."

"Where did you ever hear of Blackstone's Commentaries?"

"First out at Old Salem, where Linkern lived."

The jury sat up straighter than ever.

"Who told you?"

"An old man."

"What's his name?"

"I don't know."

"When was that?"

"This summer, about a month ago."

"Well, did you ever read Blackstone's Commentaries?"

"Yes, sir, some."

"Where?"

"In Mr. Kirby's office."

"The States Attorney?"

"Yes, sir."

"When?"

"Since that old man told me."

"How did he happen to be talking about Blackstone's Commentaries?"

"He told me that Linkern found Blackstone's Commentaries in a barl."

There was a titter in the court room.

"Did you believe him?"

"Yes, sir."

"What were you doin' out there?"

"Diggin' for treasure."

"Oh, like Tom Sawyer?"

"Yes, sir."

"And so now you're testifyin' like Tom Sawyer?"

"Yes, sir."

"Don't you dream a good deal, my boy?"

"I don't know. I think a lot."

"You think, eh? What about, for instance?"

"Everything."

"Well, tell me a few things you think about."

"The world, life, books, Shakespeare."

"Shakespeare?"

"Yes, sir."

"I suppose you've heard your father talk Shakespeare?"

"Yes, sir."

"And so you think of that?"

"I've read lots of it, too."

"Shakespeare?"

"Yes, sir."

"Uh, huh! Can you tell me the name of the play where there is a fencer?"

"'Hamlet.'"

"'Hamlet'?"

"Yes, sir. I've committed to memory the speech of the ghost."

"Well, this isn't a theater, Mitchell, so you don't need to recite."

"No, sir."

"But now tell me, has your father talked to you?"

"Yes, sir."

"Did you get from him this idea that you would be punished in the hereafter if you didn't tell the truth?"

"Yes, and not exactly either. I believe that."

"Did he talk to you to-day?"

"Yes, sir."

"What did he say?"

"He told me to do my duty, that doing my duty was more'n findin' treasure; that Linkern did his duty; that this was Linkern's county right here, and that no boy who was raised here in this town could fail to do his duty without insultin' the memory of Linkern."

"How did he come to say all that to you?"

"Because I'd stood this as long as I could. I've been in trouble about this all summer, I really started out to see Tom Sawyer, partly to get away from this, and I was troubled most of the time. And I sat here in the court room and heard the witnesses. And at noon to-day I told my pa what I knew, and he prayed with me, and told me I had to testify and that I must tell the truth, and if I didn't I'd be punished, and even if I kept still, I'd be punished and here I am."

"So here you are. Well, now to return a little, don't you have all kinds of visions and dreams, Mitchie?"

"I do."

"Wait," says my pa, "that don't go to the witness' right to testify, but only whether he's to be believed after he does testify."

"Yes," said the judge.

Then Major Abbott took another exception. There were some more questions, and finally the judge said Mitch could tell his story. So my pa settled down to business, and the jury waited anxious like. And this is the way it went.

"Where were you on the night Joe Rainey was killed?"

"Up in a tree in his yard."

"What were you doin' there?"

"Listenin' to the music."

"Were you alone?"

"Yes, sir."

"You chum with my boy, don't you?"

"Yes, sir."

"Do you know where he was that night?"

"Out to his grandpa's."

"How did you happen to be in that yard?"

"I was lonesome and I wanted to hear the music."

"Well, you go on now in your own way and tell what you saw and heard."

N

"I was lookin' from the tree through the window into the room. I could see all of you. You was singin' the 'Merry, Merry Maiden.' Just then two men came up the side-walk. I got back of some thick limbs, limbs thick with leaves, for fear they'd see me and say something and do something. Pretty soon I saw it was Joe Rainey and Temple Scott."

"What were they saying to each other?"

"They was walkin' arm in arm, friendly like. And I heard Joe Rainey say: 'I've always been a good friend of yours, Temp, and I want to be still. But you mustn't come to my house any more, especially when I'm not there. You know why, and I want you to promise.' Then Mr. Scott said, 'You're always bringin' that up, why do you? It gets me mad.' Then Joe Rainey says, 'My wife don't want you around, as far as that goes.' And Temp said, 'You don't know what you're talkin' about.' And Joe Rainey says, 'I do, and I'll go in and get her now and she'll come out here and say to you just what I say.' 'No,' says Temp, 'you'll make her say it; she must say it of her own free will.' They began to quarrel then."

"Don't say quarrel, tell us what they said."

"Well, Temp said, 'You're a liar, and nobody believes what you say.' And Joe Rainey said, 'You're another liar, and if you didn't have a pistol on you, I'd take it out of you right now. I'm goin' in for my wife.' Then he tore away from Mr. Scott and went into the house, but came right out again, and Mr. Scott began to shoot at Joe Rainey, and he fell down on the porch."

"Then what happened?"

"Then everybody in the room screamed. And somebody came out and some others and picked up Joe Rainey and carried him into the house."

"What did you do?"

"I still stayed in the tree."

"What for?"

"Well, I was kind of scared — then I wanted to see what they did with Joe Rainey. I thought they might take him into the room where they had been singin' and I could see him."

"Did you?"

"No, sir."

"Then what happened?"

"Well, while I was waiting, about ten minutes maybe, I heard some one coming from the back of the house. It was a woman."

"What did she do?"

"She came up by the porch, knelt down kind of and ran back to the rear of the house."

"What did you do then?"

"I waited a few minutes then I got down out of the tree and went over to the porch and picked up what the woman had left there."

"What was it?"

"A pistol."

"Have you got the pistol?"

"Yes, sir."

"Will you hand it to me?"

"Yes, sir."

Mitch took a pistol out of his pocket and handed it to my pa.

Then Mrs. Rainey, who was still sittin' in the court room, fainted dead away. And some women and a doctor came up and carried her out. Temple Scott was white as death, and was leanin' his head on his hand and lookin' down.

And then my pa went on.

"Where has this pistol been since that night?"

"Buried."

"Where?"

"In Montgomery's woods."

"How?"

"In a cigar box."

"Why did you bury it?"

"So it wouldn't rust — so as to hide it."

"Do you know who the woman was who put the pistol there?"

"Yes, sir."

"Who?"

"Mrs. Rainey."

"Then what did you do?"

"I still stayed in the tree."

"Did anything else happen?"

"Yes, sir."

"What?"

"In just a few minutes after Mrs. Rainey came out and left the pistol, some men came out, one of 'em was Harold Carman, and they started to look right by the edge of the porch. And one man says, 'Where is it?' and another says, 'I don't see it,' and another says, 'Is this the place?' And so they looked all around and then went back into the house."

"Then what did you do?"

"I waited until everything was all right, then I climbed down out of the tree, and got the pistol, and ran. And so I kept the pistol for a few days; but I got worried havin' it around, so I put it in a cigar box and went out to Montgomery's woods and buried it."

"And is this pistol you produced here, the same pistol you picked up, and buried?"

"Yes."

"That's all," said my pa.

Then the judge said, "We'll suspend here for a little while." Mitch started to leave the witness chair, but the judge said, "No, you must stay where you are. You stand by him, Mr. Sheriff."

Then there was a kind of noise of the people in the room changin' their seats and talkin'. And the word went around that Mrs. Rainey had died.

CHAPTER XXIII

THAT'S what had happened. She had died. Her heart went back on her. But my pa said they kept it away from the jury. And Mitch kept sittin' there lookin' pretty tired. The jury wasn't allowed to leave; but just sat there. And they passed 'em water. And the judge had gone out, probably to see Mrs. Rainey. My pa went too, and Major Abbott. Then they all came back together, and the judge got on the bench, and said to go on.

Major Abbott stood up and took off his nose glasses and began to kind of shake 'em with his hand, and he looked at Mitch, and Mitch looked at him, kind of scared, I thought. And then Major Abbott began.

"When did you first tell this story you've just told here?"

"Never before," says Mitch.

"Did you talk to the State's Attorney about it?"

"Yes, sir."

"When?"

"This noon."

"Then you did tell it before you told it here."

"Yes, sir."

"What made you say you'd never told it before, Mitchie?"

"I thought you meant in any court."

"Did you tell it to any one before you told it to the State's Attorney?"

"Yes, sir."
"Who?"
"My pa."
"When?"

MAJOR ABBOTT CROSS-EXAMINING MITCH

"This morning."
"Uh, huh. And did you tell it to any one else?"
"No, sir."
"At no time?"
"No, sir."

"At no time between the night that Joe Rainey was killed and until you told your father this morning?"

"No, sir."

"Why did you keep it to yourself?"

"For a lot of reasons."

"Didn't you know it was your duty under the law to tell what you claimed to know?"

"I kind of thought so."

"So then you were neglecting your duty and knew that you were?"

"Maybe so."

"And didn't you know that when a case is tried, the witnesses for one side are all heard together, and then the witnesses for the other?"

"Well, I know that now."

"And that it's the exception for a witness to be heard after one side of the case, the side he belongs to, has closed its testimony?"

"I know that now."

"And you waited until this case was practically over and then offered yourself?"

"Yes, sir."

"You were never subpœnaed?"

"Not in this case."

"What case were you subpœnaed in?"

"Doc Lyon."

"Did you testify?"

"No, sir."

"Why?"

"He killed hisself."

"And that let you out?"

"Yes, sir."

"You've been reading a book called 'Tom Sawyer,' haven't you?"

"Yes, sir."

"And he testified in a case and made a sensation?"

"Yes, sir."

"And you're makin' a sensation?"

"I suppose so."

"Just like Tom Sawyer?"

"Yes, sir."

"And you like it, don't you, Mitchie?"

"No, sir — I hate it."

"You're playin' the same part Tom Sawyer played?"

"I don't know."

"Did you hate it when you hid the pistol and didn't tell any one?"

"Yes, sir."

"And did you hate it up to the time you told your father?"

"Yes, sir."

"And you hate it now?"

"Yes, sir — but it's my duty."

Major Scott said to the judge, "I move to strike out those words 'but it's my duty.'" The judge said, "stricken out," then Major Abbott said:

"Just answer my question and don't volunteer anything. Now, Mitchie, isn't it true that you have been digging for treasure this summer like Tom Sawyer in the woods hereabouts, and at Old Salem?"

"Yes, sir."

"And you expected to find it?"

"Yes, sir, and we did."

"You did?"

"Yes, sir."

"Well, tell me."

"We found more'n $2,000 in Old Man Bender's cellar, after his house burned down."

"You're pretty rich, then?"

"No, the law took it away from us. It cheated to the county."

The audience broke into a laugh and the Sheriff called for order. Major Abbott resumed.

"But after that you went on hunting for treasure, you and the son of the State's Attorney?"

"Yes, sir."

"Have you ever heard that this is a community where some people have visions?"

The judge said: "That's not proper, Major Abbott." And Major Abbott said: "I thought the remark not out of form, considering that the son of the distinguished State's Attorney has illusions too."

My pa said: "This is a good place to wake up, as you'll find." And Major Abbott said: "When is waking up time?"

My pa says, "Now."

Then the people laughed and the jury and the Sheriff rapped for order again.

"Well," said Major Abbott, "did you ever deceive anybody, Mitchie?"

Mitchie tugged with his hands, and said, "Yes, sir."

"You ran away to Havana and deceived your father, didn't you?"

"Yes, sir."

"You told him you were going out to a farm to see your chum?"

"Yes, sir — and I did."

"But you were really on your way to Havana to run away to St. Louis, and see Tom Sawyer?"

"Yes, sir."

"So you did deceive your father?"

"Lookin' at it that way, I did."

"And don't you know that there is and never was such a boy as Tom Sawyer?"

"I know there is."

"How do you know that?"

"I got a letter from him."

"How do you know he wrote it?"

"It was signed with his name."

"Don't you think somebody might deceive you by signing his name to a letter?"

"Maybe."

"You never saw Tom Sawyer and never saw him write?"

"No, sir."

"And isn't it true that you don't know a thing about it?"

"I can't believe anybody would sign his name to a letter. Besides I wrote him one and it reached him, because this letter was his answer."

"And are these your reasons for believing that Tom Sawyer lives and wrote to you?"

"Yes, sir."

"Do you ever have dreams, Mitchie?"

"Lots."

"Didn't you dream about being up in this tree?"

"No, sir."

"Do you sometimes see dreams when you're not asleep — when it's day?"

"Sometimes."

"Didn't you pass the house of Joe Rainey the next morning after he was killed?"

"I believe I did."

"And wasn't it then that you picked up this pistol?"

"No, sir."

"Did you know what it means, if it was true, to see a pistol put down by a woman by this porch?"

"I think so."

"Tell me."

"Well, I thought it meant that somebody wanted to make it appear that Joe Rainey had it."

"Well, then you knew it was your duty as a good boy to tell the authorities — to tell the State's Attorney?"

"Yes, sir, I know it now."

"Didn't you know it then?"

"In a kind of way, but I was so taken up with the treasure and going to see Tom Sawyer; and I had been subpœnaed in the Doc Lyon case and I was afraid I would be subpœnaed in this case and kept here so I couldn't go away."

"Your father is a preacher, isn't he?"

"Yes, sir."

"And you have been raised to tell the truth and do your duty?"

"Yes, sir — but the flesh is weak."

"And the flesh pots are tempting," said Major Abbott right quick, "and you love treasure and love to live over the life of Tom Sawyer, a boy who never lived?"

" I can't answer that."

" Why?"

"Well, I love treasure, that is I love to find it — but I'm not livin' over Tom Sawyer's life any more than is natural."

"But it is true that you deceived your father, it is true you ran away, it is true you meant to run away from the court — all this is true?"

"Yes, sir."

"And then all of a sudden you got this idea of duty?"

"Yes, sir — by reading ' Hamlet.' "

"' Hamlet'?"

"Yes, sir, he kept foolin' with his duty, and it taught me not to."

"Did your father tell you to say that?"

"No, sir."

"I thought the great example of Lincoln had influenced you?"

"It did."

"Have you read ' Hamlet'?"

"Yes, sir, I have."

"Did he live, too?"

"Yes, sir — everybody lives that was ever wrote about."

And so Major Abbott kept cross-questioning Mitch until Mitch's mouth got dry and he had to have a glass of water. They handed it to him, and Major Abbott stood there like a hunter trappin' an animal. He was so cool and insultin' and kept comin' right after Mitch. Then he began again:

"Did you ever hear of Lincoln running away?"

"No, sir."

"Or deceiving his father?"

"No, sir."

"Or his mother?"

"His mother was dead."

"Or neglecting his duty in any way?"

"No, sir, that's the reason his example is so good."

"Well, why didn't you follow it from the beginning?"

"I told you why — I don't pretend to be good like Linkern."

"You don't?"

"No, sir, sometimes I think I'm very bad."

"Don't you think you're very bad right now to come here and tell such a story as this, after the State has closed its case, after all these weeks?"

"No, sir."

"And you knew, too, Mitchie, that it was common talk here that Joe Rainey tried to kill Temple Scott and shot at him first?"

"Yes, sir."

"And all the time you were keeping this to yourself for the sake of treasure, and in order to have your own way, and run off?"

"Yes, sir."

"And you knew that your chum's father was elected here to enforce the law, and that the guilty should be punished — all this you knew?"

"Yes, sir."

"And yet you did all that you did — all that you have told?"

"Yes, sir."

Well, then Major Abbott took another turn. He asked Mitch about the tree, whether it was a cherry tree or an oak tree, and Mitch didn't know. And he asked him how high up he was, and what the light was, and whether anybody passing couldn't see him in the tree; and how tall the woman was that put the pistol there, and how she was dressed; and where Temple Scott and Joe Rainey was when he first saw them, and if he knew Harold Carman, and what the names of the other people

were who came out; and what he did the day before,
and the week before, and the week after; and whether
he didn't fight and whip Kit O'Brien, and everything
you ever heard of from the time Mitch was a baby. It
took all the afternoon. And when Mitch got off the witness stand he was kind of weak, and his pa went up to
him and led him out, and then they locked up the jury
to keep 'em from hearin' anything. And the case went
over till the next morning.

And the next mornin' we was all down there as before.
When court took up, Major Abbott and my pa and the
judge went into the judge's room and nobody knew
what was said, the same as before, and when they came
out, Major Abbott said :

"Your honor, such unusual things have been done
in this case that I am compelled to do some myself.
I shall call the defendant to the witness stand." So he
called Temple Scott and he went up and was questioned.
He went on to say that Joe Rainey called him an awful
name, and said, "I'll kill you, and I'll get my pistol."
That Joe Rainey went in the house and came out and
fired, and that he fired then, and that he saw Joe Rainey's
pistol fall out of his hand right down by the porch some-
wheres; that then he gave himself up, and that's all he
knew.

My pa cross-questioned him awful hard for about an
hour, and asked him how he happened to have a pistol
on him. He said he was afraid of Joe Rainey on account
of the threats. And then my pa asked him why he didn't
tell his story in the first place, and not wait till Mitch
testified; and he said he didn't have to, the law didn't
require him to. And so it went, and at last he got off
the stand, and the case was closed. Then the speeches

began. My pa talked calm like, reviewin' the evidence
and so forth. And then Major Abbott got up and put a
glass of water on the table and wiped his glasses off
and said, "May it please your honor," and began.

He said it was a privilege to be here in the community
that Lincoln had hallowed, and to stand in the very
room he had stood in so many times, pleading for right
and justice, and to plead for right and justice too. And
that all his client wanted was justice; that he, as a de-
fending lawyer, was as much sworn to support the law
as the State's Attorney, and he wanted to see it enforced,
and meant to have it enforced. And with the help of
the court and the jury, it would be enforced; and his
client who had been greatly wronged and barely escaped
with his life would be freed, and could go back to his
family, and be a respected member of the community.

Then after takin' up the case about the threats and
everything, he began on Mitch.

"Think of it, gentlemen," he said, "here is a boy
who waits until the case is closed, and we have a right
to think that all they can bring against my client has
been brought, and then this boy turns up to swear
away his life. Let us be charitable, but let us be just.
I must do my duty and to do it, I must speak. Here is a
boy who confesses that he never told a word about what
he saw until yesterday. He confesses that he kept it to
himself in order that he might hunt treasure and run
away from the orders of this court; he confesses that
he has deceived his father, that he has been truant and
bad. Yes, and above all, gentlemen, he confesses he has
dreams and sees visions. He believes that a book, a
story, is true; that its characters are real; that a boy
named Tom Sawyer really lives; and he ran away to see

him; and yet they ask you to believe such a boy in the
face of this evidence. Why, you wouldn't convict a
yellow dog on such testimony — you are men who know
boys and know life and its affairs, and you know this
story is the result of a pure dream. I'll be charitable;
the boy is dreaming; he is a dreamy boy, an imagina-
tive boy, a wonderful boy — but he is not to be believed.
He never saw this at all. He was never in that tree.
The chances are he picked up this pistol the next morning
after passing there — after those people had come out
and searched for the pistol — who had heard three shots,
one of one report, and two of a different report. Why
they didn't find the pistol, God only knows; and the
witness who could testify to it is gone and here we are.
And if you ask who the other witnesses are, I confess
I don't know. We could have found their names if we
could have talked with Harold Carman; but he's gone.
And here we are, yes, in the community of Lincoln, but
in a community where cowardly people and bad people
live, like other communities. I say this because these
other people, whoever they are, should have come forward and made themselves known. It would have been
gracious if some people had come forward to tell the
truth and save; and not leave it to a boy, and him
alone, to come forward, and condemn and seek to
destroy."

Then he drew an awful picture of the gallows and the
penitentiary, and said, "Think of it. To be choked to
death on the gallows. To be for years behind prison
bars; or to go home to your old father and mother and
be blessed, and be a blessing and get back your good
name."

The jury cried, everybody nearly cried — everybody

o

but Mitch who was sittin' by me. Mitch says: "He's the dandiest liar I ever heard. I almost admire him."

Then my pa got up and of all the speeches you ever heard! The shivers just ran up and down my back. And in about five minutes he had that jury so you could knock their eyes off with a stick. He had 'em right in his hand. And he said:

"You dare to disbelieve this boy — you dare to! What does it mean? Harold Carman ran away. But where are the others? Echo answers where. Major Abbott stands up here and says that he doesn't know their names, that if Harold Carman hadn't gone away, he'd know their names, and he gets before the jury, as if he were testifying, the fact that Harold Carman is away and what he would say if he were here. He slips that in; and it's improper and he knows it. He may be a good lawyer, and he is, but he isn't a witness in this case. And suppose you accept his word and this story — what do you say? You say that in this community — call it the community of Lincoln or of the devil, there are people so low, so murderous in their hearts, that they will allow a fellow being to be prosecuted and never come forward to tell what they know, which if they told it, would clear Temple Scott before this jury on the spot. And that isn't all, if you accept this story, you say that I haven't done my duty; you say that the man you elected to enforce the law will use his power to pervert the law; will fail to get all the facts before the jury. Because you couldn't imagine that there are such witnesses who came out looking for a pistol and I wouldn't have heard it and known about it. And if I did, and didn't get them, I wouldn't be fit to be your State's Attorney, or to hold any position of trust whatever. Where is Harold Carman? It doesn't make any difference where he is. Where are the others? They're not in this town or any other town. They're not any more in being than Tom Sawyer; but they are unlike Tom Sawyer, for as a piece of fiction he is real; and as fiction, these people are unreal and don't convince."

And then my pa said: "Now, let's take up the pistol. Both sides here, everybody agrees the pistol was there. The dispute is how it got there. Consider this: Why would they come out and begin to look for a pistol? Who told them to? Who told them to look by the porch? How did they know before they got there where to look first? You've seen this pistol here — it's Joe Rainey's pistol — and here is something my astute friend overlooked; one of the cartridges is out — the rest are there — one is clear out, not shot, exploded, with the shell left, but clear out. How did that happen? Do you believe Mitchie Miller did that? Are you going to ascribe to him such devilish cunning as that? No, gentlemen, the hand that placed that pistol by the porch slipped the cartridge out first. The hand that placed that pistol there depended upon the story of three shots being fired, and in the insanity of the moment, slipped out a cartridge; and for a very good reason. It couldn't be fired at such a time. There were only two shots, according to the fair weight of the evidence; there were two bullets found in Joe Rainey's body; and those two bullets were fired by the hand of Temple Scott."

As my pa said this, his voice rose up so you could hear him all over town. John Armstrong said you could have heard him clear to Oakford. The audience just shivered when pa said this.

"Let me go on," said pa. "Let us assume Joe Rainey
comes in and runs up-stairs for his pistol and goes out.
Well, they pick him up on the porch and no pistol is
on him. Then they come out and look, but find no
pistol. What would they have done? There would
have been talk so loud about that missing pistol that
even Major Abbott could have heard it — clear over
to Jerseyville. Why was nothing said? Because the
hand that put that pistol there, the woman that put
it there was terrified. She was afraid that some one had
seen her put it there; she knew some one picked it up
that she didn't want to have pick it up — she was afraid
it would turn up against her in the wrong hands. And
she and this crowd — whoever they were — if there was
one, were afraid to go on with the evidence they had
started to manufacture. And this testimony of Mitchie
Miller is every word true. You saw his face, you heard
him, you know he wouldn't lie — and as for having
visions — if he dreamed this, he would be fit for an
asylum, and every one of you could see it — and he
would be in an asylum."

Then pa just lit into Temple Scott. He said he was a
coward, and he said when Joe Rainey asked him not to
come to his house any more, it was his business to stay
away. And that for himself he meant to stop lawless-
ness in the town. He intended to do his duty so fully
that people would be afraid to break the law and take
life. And then he said he had done his duty, and now
the jury had to do theirs, and he left the case with them.

And then the judge read a lot of instructions to the
jury and Sheriff Rutledge took 'em and locked 'em up
and we sat and waited. They was out all that day and
all that night and all the next day. And we waited.

And finally toward evening they came in and told the judge they couldn't agree. It seems, so pa said, two of the jurors was for hangin' and five for the penitentiary, and five for acquittal. So they was discharged. Temple Scott was held to the next term of court for another trial, and court adjourned.

CHAPTER ·XXIV

SO court bein' over, the town was dull again and all deserted. Watermelon rinds and newspapers was all over the court house yard. Hardly any farmers was in town. The stores seemed empty. And Mitch was quieter than I ever saw him. He didn't look well. He was reading Shakespeare; and I saw him go by with Charley King and George Heigold. I began to feel that I was losin' him.

And one day my pa said, "How would you like to go to St. Louis on the boat? Your ma and Myrtle are goin' over to visit Aunt Fannie, and Delia is goin' to take a vacation, and I think I'll take you to St. Louis. I need a rest too. Mitch and his pa are going along. Colonel Lambkin has made up a party and John Armstrong will be along. It's the *City of Peoria*, the same boat you boys tried to run away on. So we're goin'. Come down town this afternoon and I'll get you a new suit and some shoes and a hat. Get Mitch too, and I'll fit him out for the trip."

So I got Mitch and he was almost beside himself, he was that happy. And we both got suits and shoes and hats. And the next morning took the passenger train for Havaner. When we got to Oakford, John Armstrong got in, and my pa was tickled to death to see him. John says: "They didn't convict that feller?" Pa says, "No." "Wal," says John, "are you goin' to try him again?" My pa says, "I don't know. It costs the county, and the board may lay down on me. But I'll prosecute him if they stand for the appropriation."

We were all sittin' together, for we turned the seats that a way. Mr. Miller and Mitch facin' us, my pa and me in one of the seats, and John Armstrong across the aisle, after he got on. And John says, "Wal, how about that boy down that a way? Whar does he live?"

"Who?" says I.

"That boy you was runnin' away to see. Tom Sawyer, warn't it?"

And Mr. Miller said, "If he's at home, we'll see him — but he's away a lot."

"He lives in St. Louis?" says John.

"No," says Mr. Miller, "but not far from there. That's right, ain't it, Mitchie?"

Mitch says, "It's not very far, just up the river maybe a hundred miles, at Hannibal."

"Are you goin' up thar?" says John.

"No," says my pa, "we expect to see him in St. Louis."

Then John says: "You had a big court this time with that murder trial and all." Pa says, "Yes." "It does beat the world about the murders and things around here. More'n what there used to be, 'pears to me."

Then Mr. Miller began to talk about the Civil War and he said: "It's a bad thing for the country and will be for a long time. We got rid of slavery, but we took on a lot of bad things while doin' it. You see it killed off so many real Americans, the old stock, and in a few years with all these foreigners brought in to work at the mines and mills, the blood'll get mixed. And ideas about America will get mixed; and the country will forget

what it was, and what it was meant to be; and they'll
pass new laws to take care of changes. And pretty soon
you won't know the country. During the war we had
to part with liberties to carry on the war; and pretty
soon we'll part with liberties in order to manage these
new stocks. And there's a lot of corruption in the
country, people gettin' rich off'n the tariff, and that'll
make trouble."

John Armstrong was a Republican, and he didn't
agree with Mr. Miller; but my pa says, "We'll elect
Cleveland this fall and then we'll save the country."

My pa and Mr. Miller was both Democrats, but John
was a Republican and they had the best of him, bein'
two to one. But John says, "Why, they tell me that
Cleveland wears a $6\frac{7}{8}$ hat and a eighteen collar and can
drink more whisky than Joe Pink."

"Well," says my pa, "if you elect Harrison, who'll
be President — will he be President or will Blaine?
It will be Blaine, and why didn't you nominate him and
be done with it? It's because you dassent" — Then he
began to sing:

> " In Washington City, oh, what a great pity,
>   There'll be no Harrison there."

Then we kind of changed seats around and Mr. Miller
and my pa began to talk together, while John was talkin'
to Mitch and me, and pointin' out the places of interest
along the way. "Over thar," he says, "is whar Slicky
Bill Wilson used to live." "Thar's the Widow Watkins'
farm." "Right down thar is whar they held a camp
meetin' onct and converted more'n 80." And pretty
soon we went over a bridge over a clear blue stream, and
John says: "That's Salt Creek, and just down thar

about a mile old Tom Giles used to live who raised quarter horses," and so on.

Then I heard Mr. Miller tell my pa that he was goin' to lose his church for preachin' that sermon about God bein' in everything; that he was sure of it. And he didn't know what to do. He couldn't teach school and walk into the country, and he couldn't get a school to teach in town. And he was worried and said with a big family like he had on his hands, he was worried to death. That his father had had a big family and was poor and worried too, and that he could see his own children poor and havin' big families. And it looked just like the same story over and over, world without end.

By and by we got to Kilburn and the engine broke down or somethin' and we waited and waited. The conductor came in and said we'd better eat here, because he didn't know when we'd get started. So we all got off and went into the station where Mrs. Ruddy, the wife of the ticket agent, had a restaurant. She looked like a hen in the early morning. Her eyes were so quick and bright, and she kept goin' around askin' us to have things. There was a jar of jelly on the table all sealed up, and she said, "Won't you have some of the jell?" Mr. Miller said, "No, thank you." But Mitch took up the jar and tried to get the top off. It would have took a monkey wrench to get it off; so after tuggin' at it and not bein' able to budge it, he put it down. Just then she came up and said, "Do have some of the jell." Mitch began to laugh. Then pa took the jar and he couldn't get the top off either, and he put it down. She came back again and said, "Won't you have some of the jell, Mr. Armstrong?" "I don't mind if I do," says John, and he took hold of the jar. Findin' the top on, he tried to get it off. Then Mrs. Ruddy says, "Oh, the top ain't off." I believe she knew it all the time. The remark sounded just like a woman. So she went into the kitchen for an opener and came back and said she couldn't find none. Then she took the jar and got her apron about it and screwed up her face and tried her best. But the top wouldn't budge. Mitch picked up the poker by the stove and says, "Hit it with this, Mrs. Ruddy." And she says, "I'll break the jar. Just wait, I'll set it in some hot water for a bit and then it'll come off." So she disappeared with the jar. And while she was gone the conductor came in and yelled, "All aboard." And pa laid down some money and we ran for the train. Just as we was all on the platform and the train begin to move, Mrs. Ruddy came to the station door and said somethin'. John began to snicker and laugh, and says to pa, "Did you hear what she said — by God, she says it's off — let's go back and have some jell."

This time when we got to Havaner we rode in the bus, Mitch with the driver in front; and we rode pretty near down to the river's edge. And there was the *City of Peoria*, all steamed up, smoke comin' out of her stacks, and ready to go. We got on and there was Colonel Lambkin, talking to the captain and the same fat man. And when the Colonel see my pa, he smiled all over his face and got up and came over and shook his hand, and put his arm around him and says, "You look a little peaked, Hardy. We'll give you some rations that'll fatten you up. Whar's your fiddle?" he says to John. John hadn't brought it; but by and by an orchestra came on board, a man with a guitar and another with a fiddle, and so we had music all the way. Colonel Lambkin

seemed to just own the boat. We steamed off after a
bit and it was moonlight, and Mitch and me sat on deck
and watched the river, and the shores and everything
we could see. By and by Mitch said: "Do you remember when we were here and lay on top of that shed
and I told you about losin' Zueline, and that there was
somethin' else in my mind?"

"Yes," says I.

"Well," says Mitch, "you know what it was now,
don't you?"

"I think so," says I.

"Of course it was that Rainey murder and findin'
that pistol. And I'd like to ask you, Skeet, if you think
I dreamed that."

"No," says I.

"Well," says Mitch, "that lawyer did twist me around
and he did make a wonderful speech agin me. It sounded
like the characters in Shakespeare where one says
something and you think that ends it; and then the other
says something and it has a different look altogether and
seems truer than what the other one said. But I hope
to drop dead this minute, Skeet, and fall into the river
and be et by the fish if every word I said ain't as true
as the gospel."

"I know it," says I. And Mitchie says: "I wanted
to tell you that night what was on my mind; but somehow I couldn't."

Just then we became aware of voices near us, around a
kind of corner. And one voice was a woman's and
another was a man's who was talkin' kind of thick and
kept repeatin' hisself. And Mitch says, "Wait — listen."
So we listened. And this man's voice said:

"What can I do, Gwen? I'll leave it to you. Ain't

I done the right thing? Have I harmed any one? But I might have, I know myself, and I might have harmed some one as easy as that. I know what's what, and even

We Got up and Walked Past 'Em

now I do, and when I have no drinks, I know better, and you'll see I done the right thing. Why look at it — they rush on me there in all that hurry and scare and say go out where it is — where his pistol is — right by the

side of the porch and you or some of you pick it up and
bring it back in the house. What did that mean? It
meant some one knew where the pistol was before anybody seen it — and you can't make me believe that
kind of a story would wash."

Then the woman said, "It did wash."

"It washed because they didn't have me there and
try to fetch in this story. I couldn't a stood cross-
questioning a minute. That's why I say I know what
I can do."

Then the woman says: "He's goin' to be tried again
and you'd better go back and be a man. Mrs. Rainey
died and it's time Temple Scott was dead too."

"Listen," says Mitch, "did you hear that — that's
Harold Carman. Come."

We got up and walked past 'em — there he was
huddled close to a woman, the moon almost shining in
their faces. We heard the orchestra and went around
and found Colonel Lambkin dancing and everybody
havin' a wonderful time. My pa sat there so big and
powerful and I was proud to death of him.

Well, we had wonderful sleeps on board and we all
sat at the captain's table and had the most splendid
meals — fish all the time if we wanted it; and beef-
steak, and all kinds of pie and everything. Mitch and
me went into the kitchen; but just to call and say
"howdy" to Susie and the cook.

It was on a morning when we hove in sight of St.
Louis. There she was stretched further than you could
see, smoke all over her, rumblin', a scary looking mon-
ster, seemed alive, seemed full of all kinds of terrible
things, but also awful beautiful, too. We got off the boat
and there was two or three policemen there. My pa

and Colonel Lambkin talked to 'em, and then just as Harold Carman came along, the policemen took him. He scolded and made a fuss at first, but finally went along. Of course we had told pa what we heard. But pa had seen him on the boat anyway. So they just shipped him by train back to Petersburg and jailed him — I think it was for forgin' a note, but anyway it was to testify.

We got over into town, and such a sight — sloughs of people, wagons, carriages, street cars; sloughs of niggers — an awful noise everywheres. Everybody in a hurry. And Mitch says: "Tom Sawyer lives near here, and yet he was never in this town, at least if he was he writes nothing about it. And look at us. We're here. I told you everything couldn't be the same with me and you as it was with Tom and Huck. But just look, Skeet. You could take Petersburg and set it down right here in this square and nobody could find it. Why, I'll bet you this town is five miles long, as far as from Petersburg to your grandpa's farm — just think, five miles of houses." Mitch was terribly excited. And you can't imagine how funny John Armstrong looked walkin' along in St. Louis. He seemed out of place and looked strange. But my pa and Colonel Lambkin was the same as the St. Louis people, and even Mitchie's pa in a general way.

Well, we went around different places, and finally we went to a hotel about a thousand times bigger than the hotel at Havaner. The office had gilt all over it and marble pillars and a dome of blue and red glass. It must have cost millions. When we went into the dining room John Armstrong looked shamed a little like a boy standin' up to recite. And we sat down at a table.

Everybody said Colonel to Colonel Lambkin, and seemed
to know him and was awful polite to him; and the
waiters laughed at Mitch and me. And one of 'em
stood by John and says: "Baked fish, corn beef and
cabbage, brisket of beef, pork tenderloin, roast goose and
turkey and cranberry sauce." John looked stunned like,
and as if he couldn't remember what the waiter said,
and the waiter stood there waitin' for John to speak,
and finally John says, "Wal, bring me whatever's the
handiest for you."

My pa broke into the biggest laugh I ever heard him
and turned to the Colonel and said: "That story you
told me keeps goin' through my mind." And the Colonel
laughed and said, "Ain't that a good one?" By this
time the waiter had repeated to John what they had
and John said, "Wal, bring me the pork tenderloin,"
and so the rest of us had our orders in and pretty soon
we had dinner and went out.

They took us to a ball game. You had to pay to get
in. Nobody could look over or look through the fence.
It was all different from what it was at home. And
there was a pitcher there who looked like the pictures
of Edgar Allan Poe, and he could throw a curve clear
around the batter right into the catcher's hand. I saw
him. And the score was three to nothin,' not 18 to 25
as I had seen it at home.

And in the evening there was a torchlight procession
for Cleveland, and bands, and banners, and big pictures
of Cleveland. "Look at him," said John, "can't you
see he wears a 18 collar?"

"Yes," says pa, "but no $6\frac{7}{8}$ hat."

"Wal," says John, "they've fixed the picture up."
So then we went to where a man made a speech. I

forget his name, but he was a great man. And he talked
for more'n an hour, and finally got down to the fall of
Rome. And he says, "What made Rome fall? The
tariff." And John says, "That ain't the way they tell
it to me. They say Caesar made Rome fall. That's what
I've always heard. And I don't believe it was the tariff.
It couldn't be." So pa says, "Listen to him, John."
But John was kind of restless and seemed to get a
little mad. Then we went back to the hotel and went
to bed. And the next night the Colonel took all of us
to a minstrel show where they sang "Angel Gabriel."
And the next morning we got on the boat and pulled out.
For where do you suppose? Why, up the Mississippi.
Yes, we saw her when we came in, but now we saw her
for miles and miles — wonderful, more'n a mile wide.
And Mitch could hardly speak, nor could I. And where
do you suppose we was going? Why, to Hannibal, to
Tom's town. After all our waitin', after trying to run
away to see Tom Sawyer, here we was actually goin'
there with our pas, and John Armstrong, and the
Colonel.

It turned out this way. We got to Hannibal, and the
Colonel stayed with the boat and John ; and we said good-
by and went over into town. The plan was for us to
cross the river from Hannibal over to Illinois, and there
take the Wabash train to Jacksonville and then home
from there.

Mitch's pa began to make some inquiries and then
we started for some place. And pretty soon I looked up
and saw a big sign "Tom Sawyer." "Look, Mitch,"
says I. And he looked and stopped and our pas went on.
This sign was over a butcher shop. And I said : "Can
it be true, Mitch, that Tom Sawyer is keepin' a butcher

shop? Is he old enough? And would he do it? Is it in his line? He's rich and gettin' higher and higher up in the world. What does this mean?"

We followed our pas into the shop. And Mr. Miller asked a boy, "Where's Mr. Sawyer?" And the boy says, "He's in the back room." Just then a door opened and a man came in, red-faced and plump and friendly. And Mitch's pa says: "Are you Tom Sawyer?" And the man says, "That's me." And Mitch's pa says: "I'm Mr. Miller from Petersburg and this is my boy Mitchie, who wrote to you. And this is Mr. Kirby and his boy." And Tom Sawyer laughed and says: "I hope I didn't make you any trouble. I kind a heard I did. But this letter came to me from your boy, and

TOM SAWYER

I showed it to the postmaster, and he laughed; and so I thought I'd have a little fun, and I had it answered. You don't mind, do you, Mitchie?" And he kind of put his hand on Mitchie's head. "Oh," says Mitch, "there might be two persons with the same names." Tom Sawyer laughed and said, "Not in this town — anyway I had that letter written you, Mitchie, and I'm sorry now, since you took it in earnest. I meant no harm. There never was any boy here of that name, and no

P

Huckleberry Finn. It was all made up, even though it does sound real and boys believe it. How'd you like to have some bologna?" He gave both of us some. Then we talked a bit and left.

After that Mitch wasn't interested in anything. He didn't want to see the town; he just sat in front of the hotel, and our pas went around lookin' up the places where Mark Twain had been, and talkin' to folks who knew where Mark Twain got this character and the other for his book. And finally Mitch said to me: "I had a dream last night, and now I know what it means. I dreamed the engines on the trains wouldn't work any more, or wouldn't work very well, and they had to hitch horses to the engines to pull the trains. So everywhere you'd see an engine and a train and at the head of the engine a team of horses, pullin' it and the train. And it means that what was so beautiful and wonderful ain't true and won't work and after all, you're just where you were, back with horses, so to speak, and no engines; back in Petersburg, with all the wonder of Tom Sawyer gone forever." And Mitch began to cry. I didn't know what to say or to do. It was all true. There wasn't any Tom Sawyer; and this town—why we couldn't find a thing like it was in the book.

Pretty soon our pas came back and Mitch says, "When you goin' to leave?" "This afternoon," says my pa. Then Mitch says: "Let's go. I don't feel well. I want to go home."

Then Mr. Miller tried to comfort Mitch and tell him that life was full of disappointments; that everything that happens when you're a boy, happens over when you're a man, just like it, but hurts worse. And that people must dis-cip-line themselves to stand it, and make the most of life, and do for others, and love God and keep His commandments. Mitch didn't say nothin'. He just set quiet, every now and then brushin' a tear out of his eye.

When our pas had walked away, Mitch says: "Now you see the whole thing, Skeet. You've lost Tom as much as I have; but I've lost more'n you. I've lost Zueline. Both in the same summer. I don't know what I'm goin' to do. I want to go home."

And then Mitch said: "I'm mad at my pa. He ought not to brought me here. He ought not to have showed us that butcher. It's too much. He ought to have left us still believin' in the book."

CHAPTER XXV

WE crossed the river and took the train. But the fun was over. Even our pas was quiet. Mitch fell asleep in his father's arms. I couldn't talk, somehow. The summer was fading, we could see that. We could hear the crickets in the grass whenever the train stopped. Sleep was falling on the earth. The fields were still and bare. No birds sang. And the train moved on. And we were going home; and to what? No more digging for treasure; no more belief in Tom Sawyer. School would commence soon. The end of the world seemed near. I myself wanted to die; for if Mitch and me had to keep goin' through this same thing until we was old like our pas, what was the use? We got back to Petersburg; and Mitch and his pa stepped off the train and started on before we got off. They stopped after a little bit and waited for us. Then they went on; and when we got to the square, they said good-by and started for home. And my pa went to his office and took me.

When we got there we found a man in the hall, walkin' up and down. He'd been there for three days waitin' for my pa. And so pa unlocked the office and went in. The man follered and sat down. He was an old, farmer-like feller, but it seemed he lived in a town down in Pike County. He'd come up to get Nancy Allen's money, the treasure Mitch and me had found. He said he was

212

a third cousin of Nancy Allen's, and her only livin'
relative. Well, the advertisement that pa had put in the
paper for relatives had expired, and no one had turned
up to claim the money but this man. His name was Joe
Allen, and he had his proofs with him that he was
Nancy Allen's third cousin. He said his wife was dead;

COUNTING THE TREASURE

that he had no children; that he did a little draying in
his town; that he wanted to get a new wagon and a
span of mules, cost about four hundred dollars; and this
money came in awful handy for him. Then he looked
around the room and saw pa's books. And he said that
he never had such schoolin', that he wanted schoolin'
and never had and that if he'd had it, he'd been a
lawyer too, may be instead of running a dray. And then

pa went over to the safe and got the money, for he hadn't turned it in to the treasury yet. He counted the money and left it on the table. And then the man was interested in how it was found. And pa told him and says: "This is one of the boys that found it; this is my boy. And the other boy is preacher Miller's boy, one of our best citizens," meaning Mr. Miller, of course, and not Mitch. "And they're poor, and Mitch is one of the most wonderful boys you ever saw — very smart and reads all kinds of books."

Then the man took the money and counted it and put it in his pocket. But my pa says, "We'll have to do a lot of things about papers and receipts and things before you can have the money." So the man took it out and put it on the table; and then he counted it again. And finally he separated it and handed part of it to my pa and says, "Count it." So pa did. And the man says, "Is that a thousand dollars? I don't reckon very well." "Yes," says pa. "It's a thousand dollars and ten dollars more." And the man took the ten-dollar bill and put it on the other pile.

"Here," says the man, "take this thousand dollars and take your fee out of it."

My pa says, "No — you don't owe me nothin'. The county pays me for my work, and it wouldn't be right, and you need it more than I do."

"Well," says the man, "what I meant was for you to take your fee out of it, and then split the difference between these two boys."

"No, you don't owe them nothing," says pa. My heart sank. I said "I —," and was about to say something, I don't know what; but pa winked at me to keep still and says, "This money is yours, and if you'll come

with me, we'll attend to everything, and you can take
it and go home."

Then the man said: "But you say one of these boys
is poor and is smart. And I know what it is to be poor
when you're a boy, even if you're not smart, as I warn't;
and to want to get up in the world and not be able to,
as I have. And I know what it is to feel it all your life,
what you didn't have when a boy. And, as I said, I
have no one in the world but myself, and I don't need
nothin'; and after I buy this wagon and span of mules
then I'll have more'n six hundred dollars to lend out.
It's enough for me. It makes me well fixed, with my
house, which I own. And here I have a good chance to
do good to a couple of boys who found the money, and
may use their sheer to make men of 'em — and you just
take this $1,000 and if you don't want any of it, give it
all to 'em."

Then he said, "Where is this boy, Mitch Miller? I'd
like to see him. You say he's a smart boy." So my pa
says, "Run up and get him." And I ran — ran all the
way — breathless to tell Mitch that we had struck it
at last. When I got to his house, no one was there but a
woman doin' the washin'. She didn't know where any
of the family was. That she saw Mitch go away with his
fishin' pole. So I ran back and told pa, and he says,
"Never mind — let it go — it's just as well." While I
was gone, the man and pa seemed to have come to terms.
Pa was goin' to take the thousand dollars. He did and
gave the rest to the man and he said good-by and went.

Then pa turned to me and says: "I'll put this in the
safe. But mind you, you're not to say a thing to Mitch
or any one about it. It will be a Christmas gift, which
ain't far off. And if you tell, I'll keep your half for my

fee. I'll find it out, sure, if you tell. Promise me now not to tell." And I promised.

Then pa locked the money up in the safe. And he said: "Go home, now; and tell your ma I'll be home for supper. She's back from her visit and will be glad to see you."

So I went home.

CHAPTER XXVI

THERE was days in here that I kind of forget. I remember Mr. Miller gave Mitch a watch which he had always promised him, and it looked good, but didn't run very well. So he was goin' to old Abe Zemple, which was a mechanic, to fix it. But it seemed to run worse, if anything. One thing that happened there was this: Old Zemple had a clock all apart, the wheels and springs scattered all over the bench. Mitch saw this and for fun he put a extra wheel on the bench with the rest. So when Old Zemple was puttin' the clock together again he couldn't find no place for this wheel; and finally he just left it out,

ABE ZEMPLE

and of course the clock run, havin' all the wheels back in it that really belonged to it. He went around town braggin' about puttin' a clock together with one wheel left out, and it was just as good as if it had all the wheels, and that showed that the factory didn't know about clocks.

But it happened that in fixin' Mitch's watch, old Zemple had left out a little pin, just a little pin that you could hardly see, and Old Zemple found it out and put the pin in, and then the watch run. Old Zemple told Mr. Miller about leavin' the wheel out of the clock, and Mr. Miller said, "How do you explain it, Abe? You leave a big wheel out of a clock and it runs; and you leave a little pin out of a watch and it won't run? Somethin's wrong. Look into it, Abe. For I've noticed about people that when they try to get somethin' extra into their lives, and fuss around like you did with this wheel, tryin' to find a place for it, that they don't need it, and do all right without it; and on the other hand, other people lose somethin' so little it don't seem to count, and yet they can't get along without it. But also sometimes a man thinks he's improved on creation by leavin' somethin' out of his life, or gettin' rid of somethin' in society, and it turns out that it didn't belong there, just like this wheel. We get fooled a good deal; for you know, my boy put that extra wheel on your bench." And then Old Zemple said, gettin' mad — "Some boys have lost pins, or never had any. Their fathers don't raise 'em up right." And Mr. Miller said: "This town is just full of wheels that have nothin' to do with the clock. They either belong somewhere else, or they are left-overs of other times — like Henry Bannerman," referring to the man that spent all day every day walkin' up and down on the stone floor back of the pillars of the court house.

I want to come back to Mitch's watch. But first I remember it was about now that a troupe came to

town playin' Rip Van Winkle, and Mr. Miller and my
pa took Mitch and me to see it. And as we came back
home, pa said to Mr. Miller: "Henry Bannerman is a
kind of Rip Van Winkle — a extra wheel — he's been
asleep ten years, anyway." So Mitch and me began to
beg for the story about Henry Bannerman, which was
that he drank until he had a fever and when he came out
of the fever, he was blurred like and not keen like when
he could recite Shakespeare and practice law fine. So
pa said that onct when Henry first began to practice
law again after comin' out of the fever, he had a little
office in the court house and Alcibiades Watkins came
in to see him about a boundary fence, and sat down and
told Henry about it, takin' about an hour. When
Alcibiades finished, Henry says, "Tell it to me over;
it's a long story and important and I want to get it right."
So Alcibiades told it over. And then Henry says, "You
came to consult me, did you?" Alcibiades said "yes."
"Well," says Henry, "I'll have to charge you — I'll
have to charge you two dollars for the advice." And so
Alcibiades took out two dollars and handed it to Henry
and waited for the advice. And Henry said: "Well,
Alcibiades, I have listened to you for two hours about
this boundary, and the boundary fence, and I don't
know a thing about it, and my advice to you is to go
and see Mr. Kirby who can understand it and is a good
lawyer." So Alcibiades said, "Well, I know, but I
came to you for advice." "Yes," said Henry, "I know
you did, and I have give it to you — go and see Mr.
Kirby — he's a good lawyer and will tell you what
more to do and how to do it. You see I'm not a barris-
ter — I'm just a solicitor."

So Mr. Miller and my pa talked, which was as much

fun almost as the show. They seemed to know everything and to kind of stand back of Mitch and me, next to
God, or somethin' strong that could keep any harm
away.

But to come back to Mitch's watch. George Heigold
had a piece of lead with printing letters on one side, in
copper. They called it a stereotype, and it would print.
And he wanted to trade Mitch for the watch, so he
offered his stereotype; and as Mitch was crazy about
printin' and books, Mitch traded and was glad of the
chance. But when Mr. Miller found it out, he said:
"What did you do that for? That lead stereotype ain't
worth nothin' — and here you have traded off your watch
which I gave you. You know, I think you are goin' to
be a author — for authors give their time and everything
they have to print things — and this looks like the key
to your life, and a sign of what your life is goin' to be.
So I think I'll begin with you and put you in the office
of the *Observer* to learn the printer's trade, like Franklin."

Of course this stereotype would print; and Mitch
printed with it a good deal, but as it always printed the
same thing, the fun soon died down, and Mitch really
wished he had his watch back.

So that's how Mitch began to set type and help run
a newspaper. The editor was Cassius Wilkinson, and a
good deal of the time he was in Springfield, and the rest
he was talkin' politics or gettin' drunk. So that the paper
just run itself. The foreman was Dutchie Bale, who
used to go to the farm papers or the Chicago papers and
just cut great pieces out of 'em and set 'em in type for
the paper; and as the editor didn't care, and Dutchie
didn't care what went into the paper, Mitch had a
chance to write for the paper himself; and also Mr.

Miller slipped in some wonderful things; and people began to say that the paper was lookin' up. While Mr. Wilkinson, the editor, smiled and took the compliments give him just like he deserved 'em. And onct Mitch printed one of his poems about Salem, where one of the verses was:

> Down by the mill where Linkern lived,
> Where the waters whirl and swish,
> I love to sit when school is out,
> Catchin' a nice cat fish.

I don't believe Mitch worked on the newspaper more'n a week or ten days, but lots happened; and I went down to see him a good deal to hear Dutchie Bale talk and swear. He swore awful, especially on press day; for the press nearly always broke down just as they started to print. Then Dutchie would turn loose:

"Look at the old corn-sheller, look at the old cider mill, look at the junk (all the time puttin' in the awfulest profanity). Here he's over at Springfield, and me runnin' the paper and tryin' to print a paper on a grindstone like this. I'm goin' to quit — I've had enough of this (more terrible profanity)."

Mitch would be standin' there half scared and half laughin', and another printer named Sandy Bill would be sayin': "Why don't you tighten that bolt, Dutchie?" Then Dutchie would crawl under the press and start to do what Sandy said, but findin' that the bolt was all right, he'd crawl out again and maybe see Sandy kind of laughin'. So thinkin' Sandy was foolin' him, they'd begin to quarrel; and maybe, it would end with Dutchie throwin' a monkey wrench at Sandy and rushin' out of the room. He'd come back later, for you couldn't really drive him off the place ; and maybe after a hour or two the paper would be printed.

Well, Mr. Miller had wrote a long poem about the Indians, and he began to print it, and then somethin' happened. A man named Pemberton, which they called the Jack of Clubs, and a man named Hockey, which they called "Whistlin' Dick," had an awful fight by the corner store ; and Mitch wrote up the fight for the paper, the editor bein' in Springfield, and Dutchie not carin' what was printed. Mitch called 'em human wind-mills ; and when the paper came out, everybody in town began to laugh and the papers sold like hot cakes. Mr. Wilkinson was in Springfield and had nothin' to do with it ; but Whistlin' Dick thought Mr. Wilkinson had wrote the piece and put it in. So he kept goin' to the depot waitin' for Mr. Wilkinson to get off the train from Springfield. When he did, which was in a day or two, he went right up to Mr. Wilkinson and hit him, and then proceeded to lick him until he had enough, and got up and ran ; though he was sayin' all the time that he didn't write the piece and didn't know nothin' about it. Then Mr. Wilkinson came to the office and read the piece and Dutchie told him that Mitch wrote it. And that ended Mitch as an editor. He was afraid to go back to the office anyway, in addition to bein' fired.

CHAPTER XXVII

MITCH was now a changed boy and every one could see it. He didn't come around as much as he used to. At first Mr. Miller set him to work to learn the printer's trade as I have told. That kept him away from me; but after he lost the job, still I didn't see him like I used to. I looked him up a good deal, but he was mostly quiet. He didn't want to fish, or to swim, or to go out to the farm — he just read, Shakespeare and other books; lying in the grass by his house. And he wouldn't come down to see me much, because he said it made him think of Little Billie. And Zueline had gone away with her mother, they said to Springfield; and if she'd been home, Mitch couldn't have seen her anyway. I was terrible lonesome without Mitch and the days dragged, and I kept hearin' of him bein' off with Charley King and George Heigold and it worried me.

Harold Carman had been put in jail, and then let out on bond, which held him to testify in the Rainey case. And one day Mitch came to me and says: "I'm really caught in this law. I've been to see your pa. I thought I'd told my story once and that would do; but he says there'll be a new jury that never has heard about the case or what I know; and I'll have to tell it all over again. And with Harold Carman to tell about their tryin' to get him to say he found a pistol, and my story, they can convict Temple Scott. So I'm caught; and if we had ever so much to do, and ever so much treasure to find, or trips to take, I'd have to put it aside for this here law and testifyin'. And if they knew how I hated it, they'd never ask me if I didn't like it, and like makin' a sensation and actin' the part of Tom Sawyer."

" Pinafore " was played at last, and we all went, but when my pa sang the " Merry, Merry Maiden and the Tar," Mitch got up and left the hall, because, as he said to me afterward, it brought back that awful night when Joe Rainey was killed. It must have affected others that way too; that and the death of Mrs. Rainey, who had a part in the show. For they only played two nights, instead of three, which they intended. Not enough came to make it worth while.

Then one night I went up to see Mitch and the house seemed quieter. The girls was playin' as before, but not so wild. Mr. Miller was readin' to Mrs. Miller, English history or somethin'; but Mrs. Miller looked kind of like she was tryin' to pay attention. She didn't act interested and happy like she used to. Mitch told me then that his pa had been let out of the church; that while we was gone to St. Louis the trustees met and decided that they wanted a minister who would put a lot of go into the church and get converts and make things hum; that the mortgage on the church had to be met and they couldn't meet it without gettin' more people interested in the church and church work. That may have been all true; but just the same everybody said that Mr. Miller was let go because he preached that sermon about God bein' in everything, which he didn't mean except just as a person talks to hisself. He was dreamin', like Mitch, when he said it.

So Mr. Miller was goin' to Springfield to see what he could do about gettin' to sell books or maps or atlases, and quit preachin' till a church turned up, or preach a little now and then, and marry folks when he could, and preach at funerals. I heard Mr. Miller say to my pa that he was worried about Mitch; that Mitch talked in his sleep and ground his teeth, and talked about engines and horses and findin' pistols and treasure, and ridin' on steamboats, and about Zueline and Tom Sawyer. And he said he'd tried to get him to go out to the farm with me and ride horses and get a change, but he wouldn't. He just read Shakespeare until they hid the book; and then they found him readin' Burns; and once Ingersoll's Lectures, which they also took away, because Mr. Miller thought Mitch was too young.

About this time I was about a third through readin' the Bible to earn that five dollars that grandma had promised me. And Mitch asked me what I thought, and I said I didn't understand it much; but in parts it was as wonderful as any book. And Mitch says, "Do you know what the Bible is?" "No," I says; "what is it?" "Why," he says, "the Bible is the 'Tom Sawyer' of grown folks. I know that now; so I don't have to go through the trouble of findin' it out after I'm grown up and depended upon it for a long while. There's the sky and the earth, and there are folks, and we're more ᴄ_____al to each other, and there's something back of o_____ ᴵieve when you die, you're asleep — sound ____ ᴛt know it. And why we should wake ____ ᴏ to sleep forever is more than my ____ ᴵ in the world knows."

____ his talk. He was so earnest

____ ᴏ sure.

One night when I was up to Mr. Miller's, it came up somehow what we was goin' to do when we was grown up — Mitch and me — and Mrs. Miller thought we should be taught somethin' to earn a livin' by; and that the schools instead of teachin' so much, and teachin' Latin and Greek, which nobody used, should teach practical things.

And Mr. Miller said, "Look out! That's comin' fast enough; it's on us already. For back of the schools are the factories and places that always want workers, and they're already usin' the schools to turn out workers, boys who don't know much, or boys who know one thing. And it makes no difference what happens to me — it's just as much or more to know how to enjoy life and to enjoy it, as it is to be able to earn a livin'. If you earn a livin' and don't know how to enjoy life, you're as bad off as if you know how to enjoy life, but can't make a livin', or not much of one. Look here, you boys: Anything that gives you pleasure, like Greek and Latin, stories, history, doin' things, whatever they are, for the sake of livin', are worth while. And you let yourselves go. And don't be molded into a tool for somebody's use, and lose your own individuality."

And that's the way he talked. And then he said it was all right to dig for treasure if we wanted to, and to want to see the Mississippi River and see Tom Sawyer, and he didn't blame us a bit for anything we had done. "Yes," he says, "I'll take you to Springfield to-morrow; ask your pa, Skeet, and come along."

I did; and the next morning we took the train for Springfield; and here was a big town, not as big as St. Louis, but awful big. The capitol was bigger'n any building in St. Louis, with a great dome and a flag

And Mr. Miller took us out to see Lincoln's monument.
Just when we got there, two men in overalls came runnin' from the back of the tomb and said a man — an
old soldier — had just killed himself with a knife. So
we ran around and found him lyin' in a lot of blood.
The men came back and took a bottle of whisky out
of his pocket, and a writing which said that the prohibition party had been defeated, and if it had won
he couldn't have got whisky; and so he killed himself
because the prohibition party had been defeated. And
Mitch says, "What a fool idea! If he wanted the prohibition party defeated, why did he drink and buy whisky;
and if he drank and carried whisky in his pocket, why
did he want the prohibition party to win, and kill himself because it lost? He was crazy, wasn't he, pa?"

And Mr. Miller said, "Not necessarily — that's sense
as things go in the world. Some people want whisky
done away with so they can't get it their own selves, and
when they can't get a law for that, it disappoints 'em,
and they keep on drinkin' because they're disappointed,
or kill themselves because their disappointment is too
much. For you can depend upon it that any man that
gets his mind too much fixed on any idea is like a cross-
eyed man killin' a steer with a sledgehammer; he hits
whar he's lookin', and hits wrong. Lincoln had a way of
holdin' to an idea without the idea draggin' him down
and away from everything else."

They had carried the dead man off, so we went into
the tomb to see the curiosities. And there was more
things than you could see: All kinds of flags and framed
things, pictures and writing and showcases with pistols,
and all sorts of trinkets, bullets, and knives; and a pair
of spectacles which Linkern had wore, and a piece of a

rail he had split, and books he'd read, and a piece of ribbon with his blood on it the night he died, and a theater program and lots of other things.

Then we went outdoors and looked up at the monument, and it made me dizzy to see the clouds sail over the top of it. And there was a figure of Linkern in iron, and of soldiers in iron charging, and horses in iron; besides mottoes cut in the stone and in iron. Then we went around to the back again where the old soldier had killed himself. They had the blood wiped up now. So we looked through the iron bars where a stone coffin was, but Linkern wasn't in there, Mr. Miller said. For once they had tried to steal him, and got the lead coffin out, and clear down the hill that we could see; but they caught 'em. And after that they dug way down and put Linkern there, and then poured mortar or concrete all over him, clear up to the top; then laid the floor again and put this marble coffin there, which was a dummy and had nothin' in it. So now nobody could get Linkern forever and ever.

And then we came around in front again, and Mr. Miller looked up at the statue of Linkern and began to study it, and he says: "I brought you boys to Springfield and out here to learn and to get things into your mind. You'll remember this trip as long as you live. It's the first time you've ever been here, and you'll be here lots of times again, maybe; but you'll always remember this time. Now, just look at Lincoln's face and his body and tell me how anybody could see him and not see that he was different from other men. Look how his face comes out in the bronze and becomes wonderful, and then think if you can how a handsome face would look in bronze — just the difference between a wonderful cliff or mountain side, and a great, smooth, perfect bowlder. And yet, boys, that man went right around here for twenty years, yes and more, all around this town, all around Petersburg, up at Old Salem, all over the country, practicing law, walking along the streets with people, talkin' with 'em on the corners, sittin' by 'em by the cannon stove in the offices of the hotels, sleepin' in the same rooms with 'em, as he did up at Petersburg at the Menard House, when the grand jury had the loft and they put Lincoln up there too, because there was no other place to put him."

AT LINCOLN'S MONUMENT

"The Menard House," says Mitch; "do you mean that hotel there now?"

"The very same," said Mr. Miller; "didn't you know that?"

"No," says Mitch.

"Well, that shows you; you're like the people who lived when Lincoln did, they didn't know him, some of them; and now you don't know the places he went to and the country he lived in; and you'd never have gone to Old Salem, if you hadn't gone there for treasure — would you, Mitch?"

Mitch said he didn't know, maybe not.

"Well," said Mr. Miller, "if you find Lincoln while

tryin' to dig up a few rotten dollars, it's all right anyway. Now, boys, look here, it seems an awful time to you since Washington lived, since the Government was founded — but it isn't. We're all here together, and when you get to be old men, you'll see that you were born and lived in the beginning of the republic. How will it look hereafter? Do you want to know — take a history and look at it now. Let's see! Washington had just been dead ten years when Lincoln was born; Lincoln had been dead eleven years when you were born. When Lincoln was born, the Government had been founded just twenty-three years, was just a little more than of age. It wasn't but just eighty years old when Lincoln became president. Why, these figures are nothing. Think about it. When did Juvenal live? About 42 A.D. When did Virgil and Horace live, and Caesar and Augustus and Domitian? What does forty years here or there mean when you're lookin' back over hundreds of years or a thousand? And so I say, you boys were born in the beginning of the republic, not a hundred years after it was started, and if either of you ever get your names into the history, there it will be beside Lincoln, and not far from Washington — for you were born ten years after Lincoln died and not a hundred after Washington. Well, there you are. You're young and the republic is young; and the chance is before you to do for the country and help out, for we're havin' bad times now, and they'll be worse. After every war, times is bad, and we're goin' to have other wars and worse'n ever."

Then Mr. Miller said: "There's two kinds of men — at least two. One that thinks and one that acts; or one that tells people what to do, and others that listen and do it, or else have thought it out first themselves, and do it. Well, look at Lincoln up there. Here he was over at Old Salem running a store, surveyin'; then in politics a little, then a lawyer; but mostly for twenty years he was thinkin' about the state of the country, slavery and things; and he thought it all out. Then they elected him president, and he acted out what he thought."

"Well, don't you suppose he could have got rich practicing law or tradin' in land? He was a good lawyer — none better! Why didn't he get fees and save and buy land during the twenty years he practiced law? Because his mind was set on the country, on how to make the country better, on being a shepherd of the people. The man who thinks of money all the time, thinks of himself; and the man who thinks of the country and wants to help it is thinking of what can be done for people and how the country can find treasure in having better people, and better laws, and better life and more of it. Yes, sir, boys, you'll find somewhere that Lincoln said his ambition was to be well thought of by his fellow citizens, and to deserve to be. And it never occurred to him that he could do that by getting money."

"Don't you boys think I'm lecturin' you for huntin' for treasure, or that I want either of you to grow up and be as poor as I am. I don't. I want you to have sense and provide for yourselves; Lincoln did that; he really had plenty after he got fairly started. But on the other hand, gold as gold I hate, and I see it getting power in this country. Why, it has it now. Look at Lincoln's face, what do you think he'd think of what's happened since the war — the robbery, ruin and conquest of the

South, the money grabbing and privilege grabbing at the North, the money deals in New York, the money scandals everywhere — the treasure-hunting everywhere — and not a big man left in the country; none of the old, fine characters left who built their lives on foundations of wisdom and service and makin' the country better — none of these left to come forward and take the country out of the hands of these vultures, wolves, hyenas. And what are we going to have? Is money goin' to be the master in this country, or is man goin' to be? I hate it — I hate it as Lincoln hated it when he asked whether the dollar or the man should be put first. And I hate it because it is brainless, spiritless. It cares for nothing but itself. It is a snake that swallows and sleeps and wakes to eat again. It is a despot; it is without love, genius, morality. It is against people, against God, against the country. It is as wicked as Nero, as gluttonous as a cormorant; and it makes cowards, slaves, lick-spittles of some of the best of men. In this country, intended to be of free men, where men could grow and come to the best that is in them, already we find these laws and principles mocked — by what? By gold, by riches; and we find talented men and good men compelled to step aside for rich men; and rich men held higher than good and useful lawyers, preachers or anything else. Well, there's Lincoln: and if never again in the history of this country a rail-splitter, a boy who worked up from nothing with his hands and his mind, comes to rulership, still there's Lincoln, on whom no rich man could frown; and no big-bellied capitalist could patronize or ignore or make step aside. Why, it's great — it makes me happy, it gives me hope. And I can see for ages and ages the face of Lincoln on books, on coins, on monuments; until some day his face will be the symbol of the United States of America, when the United States of America has rotted into the manure piles of history with Tyre and Babylon, as it will if it doesn't turn back and be what Lincoln was: a man who worked and thought, and whose idea was to have a free field, just laws, and a democracy where to make a man and not make a dollar is the first consideration."

And then Mr. Miller said: "Yes, this is a great monument and Lincoln was a great man. You see when all the sap-heads and poets down in New England and all over was hollerin' for nigger equality and to give the nigger a vote and to marry him, and give him the same right as anybody, Lincoln just kept cool; and he didn't even emancipate the nigger until he had to in order to win the war. It was to win the war, understand. He wasn't swept off his feet by anybody, orators or poets or yawpers — nobody. But you'll see when you grow up what the difference is between not havin' the nigger for a slave and allowin' him to vote and marry you; and you'll see that what Lincoln said when he went over the country debatin' with Douglas, speakin' at Havana, and right here in Springfield and at Petersburg, too, he said to the last and acted on to the last. It was after the war and after Lincoln was dead that these here snifflers and scalawags got into power and pushed it over until they gave the nigger the vote and all that. And if this country goes to pieces because the good breeds have been killed off and die off, and the country is run by the riff-raff, then Lincoln, say five hundred years from now, will stand greater than he is to-day, unless the world can then see that the nigger should have been kept a slave, so as to let the wise and the intelligent have time to think better and work better for the good of the country. For, boys, you can put it down that a country ain't good that is run on the principle of countin' noses, and lettin' everybody have a say just because he walks on two legs and can talk instead of barkin' or waggin' his tail." And so Mr. Miller went on.

Then Mr. Miller said damn, or that something could be "damned." And Mitch says, "Pa, did you know you swore?" And Mr. Miller says: "I shouldn't have, and don't you follow my example. But sometimes I get so mad about the country."

So we had seen the monument and walked away; and when we got a long way from it, we turned around and looked at it for the last.

Then Mr. Miller said he was glad he was out of the church, that he had tried to do certain things, but they wouldn't let him, and kept him in a groove. And now he was going to sell atlases and geographies, and be a free man, and maybe write a book. And he said: "The idea seems to be that goodness, spirituality, is church. It isn't, and it never was; it wasn't when the Savior came; He found goodness and spirituality in a lot of things, in a free life, in the freedom of out-doors, and not in the synagogues. Now, boys, believe in the Bible, in the Savior — I mean that; but don't let that belief make you into a membership with those who live for denial, for observation of injunctions, for abstinence from life, more or less, for solemnity, for religion as business, and business as religion, and religion for business. This is not goodness — not spirituality. Lincoln was good and spiritual — he believed in the mind and he used it. Wisdom, beauty, play, adventure, friendship, love, fights for the right, and for your rights, travel, everything, anything that keeps the mind going; and kindness, generosity, hospitality, laughter, trips down the Mississippi, making cities beautiful and clean, having fun, — all these things are spirituality and goodness. They are religion — they are the religion of the Savior. They will make America; and they ought to be Americanism."

So Mr. Miller went on. I can't remember half he said, but it was plain he was worked up. Losin' his church or somethin' had set his thoughts free; and everything considered, I think he wanted to give us some ideas about things. And so after lookin' at Linkern's home, a frame house, not very big, not fine, but a good house; and lookin' at the furniture and things he had, we took the train back to Petersburg.

CHAPTER XXVIII

I COULD see plainer and plainer that I was losin'
Mitch. There was somethin' about having this
business together of huntin' for treasure that kept
us chums; and now that was over and if we didn't
get something else, where would we end up? Mitch
said that the trip to Springfield had cured him of being
mad at his pa for takin' us to Hannibal to see Tom
Sawyer the butcher. And he said: "Suppose you was
at Old Salem fishin' and you had a can of worms for bait,
or thought you had, and you was really out of worms.
Which would be better, to set there and think you had
bait and go on believin' that until you began to catch
fish and needed lots of bait and found you hadn't none,
or to find out you hadn't none all of a sudden and then
go get some in time for the fishin' that got good? And
so, wasn't it better to find out that Tom Sawyer didn't
live and find it out suddenly than to go along being
fooled until something serious happened, and be a fool
to the end, and maybe lose some good chance?" What
I wanted to tell Mitch was that our case was real, that
we had found treasure and would get it on Christmas;
but I had promised my pa I wouldn't tell, and I didn't.
I only said to Mitch: "We're just as sure to get treasure
as the sun shines." And Mitch said: "Maybe, but not
real treasure, not money, not jewels, or things like that."
As I said, I was surely losin' Mitch, for he was goin'

considerable now with Charley King and George Heigold.
I don't know what he found with them to like; only
they were older and as it turned out, he did things
with them that he and I never did. I tried my best to
hold on to him, but couldn't. Sometimes I'd think I wasn't
losin' him, that it was just fancy. Just the same things
wasn't the same. The Miller family wasn't the same;
there wasn't as much fun up there; and now Mr. Miller
was away a good deal selling atlases; and sometimes
when I was there of evenings Mrs. Miller would be
sittin' alone, no one reading to her, and the girls kind of
walkin' the rooms, and Mitch a good deal away of
evenings, not home like he always was before.

You see I had a pony all the time; but pa loaned
him here and there, and sometimes took him out to pasture across the river to a farmer's and that's how it was
I didn't ride him sometimes out to the farm. But now
he was in the barn, and as I didn't have Mitch, I rode
about the country by myself. And once went out to the
farm for a few hours, comin' back to town in a gallop
all the way, to see how quick I could make it.

Finally I thought I'd go out to the farm on my pony
and stay for a few days, and go camping with my uncle
over to Blue Lake. I was goin' the next day and was out
under the oak tree when Mitch came along. He seemed
stronger, bigger, more like Charley King and George
Heigold; there was somethin' about him kind of hard.
He seemed as if he'd fight easier; he was quick to talk
back, he seemed to be learnin' about things I didn't
know. There was a different look in his eyes. He was
changed. That's all I know. Mitch set down in the
grass and began to make traps out of timothy to catch
crickets. Somebody had taught him that. His face

began to change. He began to look friendlier and like himself again, except he looked older and like he knew more. And then he began to talk:

"Skeet," he says, "I'm not Tom Sawyer, and I never was; never any more than you was Huckleberry Finn. I know who I am now. Do you?"

"No," says I. "Who are you?"

"Well, I'll tell you, Skeet — I'm Hamlet."

"Hamlet — who was he?"

"Well," says Mitch, "he was a prince."

"Well, you ain't," says I.

"No, I ain't. But Hamlet could be just like me and not be the preacher's son; and because he wasn't wouldn't make him different. Yes, sir, I'm Hamlet. I've read the play and thought about it a lot. And I know now who I am. And you, Skeet, are Horatio."

"Who was he?" says I.

"He was Hamlet's friend, just as you are my friend. And as far as that goes, there was never any persons more alike in this world than you and Horatio. You are good and steady, and don't change, and you are a good friend, you have got sense, and you have no troubles of your own, and so you can listen to mine, as Horatio listened to Hamlet's."

"What troubles have you?" says I.

"Lots," says Mitch, "that is general troubles — of course Zueline and this here court worries. I've got to testify again. I'm tangled up just like Hamlet was, and I want to get away like he did, and I can't. And it teaches me that it ain't because I'm a boy that I can't get away, for Hamlet was a man and he couldn't. He was getting old, most thirty, and he couldn't do any more with his life than I can with mine — not as much, maybe."

"And yet you say he was a prince."

"Yes, but what difference did that make? Did you ever see a chip get caught in a little shallow in the river in the reeds; and then see it get out of the shallow by the current changing or somethin', and then see it start down the river all gay and free, and run into some brush floatin', or get thrown against the logs to one side of the dam and held there? Well, Hamlet was a prince, and he was just a chip caught by the dam and couldn't budge and kept tryin' to and couldn't. This is what my pa says the play means; but also I can see it for myself. I keep readin' it and it gets clearer. And pa says it will never make any difference how old I get, the play will be wonderfuler and wonderfuler, and is to him; and that finally I'll wonder how any man could ever write such a thing."

"But didn't Shakespeare — he wrote it, didn't he? — get it out of some history?"

"Of course," says Mitch, "and didn't Linkern live, and right here in this town, as you might say? But suppose somebody could write up Linkern and use the very things that Linkern did and said, not as we hear 'em around here, wonderful as they are; but write 'em up so that you'd know what Linkern really was and why and all about it. For that matter, take Doc Lyon. We know he was a lunatic, but why, and what for, and just what it means to be a lunatic, I don't know and no one will know until some Shakespeare writes him up. For that matter, some folks think that Hamlet was a lunatic."

"Well, you ain't, Mitch," says I.

"No more than Hamlet was. He just was troubled and his mind kept workin', and that's me. But what would you say if I was the son of Joe Rainey and Mrs. Rainey?"

"How do you mean?" says I.

"Well, suppose I was their son, and suppose I knew that Mrs. Rainey, my mother, wanted Joe Rainey, my father, dead, and put it into Temple Scott's mind to kill my father, Joe Rainey; and then Temple Scott did kill him, and then Mrs. Rainey, my mother, put a pistol down so as to make it seem that my father, Joe Rainey, had carried a pistol. Suppose I was their son and was up in the tree and saw what I saw, what would I do?"

"Then you'd have to testify," said I.

"You don't know what you're sayin', Skeet. You don't see that I love my father, and he's been murdered; and I love my mother, and she has really murdered him. And if I testify against my mother, I get her hanged; and if I don't testify against her, then I wrong my father that I love; my mother goes free, and sometimes I hate her, because she is free, and my father has been robbed of his life, and I do nothing to punish her and Temple Scott for taking his life away. That's the worst of it; or maybe it's just as bad because I'm tangled in law and can't do what I want to do — can't be free to hunt treasure, we'll say, or do what I want to. Don't you see what a fix I'm in? Then suppose with findin' out what my mother is, the whole world changes for me — I get suspicious of my girl, and won't marry her and everything goes bad and finally I get killed myself, after killin' Temple Scott who's married my mother, we'll say, and in a way cause my mother to die too."

"Well, of course all this can't be," says I, "for you're not the Raineys' son; — they're both dead anyway; and Temple Scott will probably be hanged, and no one

will kill you — you'll grow up and get married — not
to Zueline —"

"No," says Mitch, "never to her. For I ain't suspicious of her — I'm just done with her, just like Hamlet
was done with Ophelia. I know her as he knew Ophelia,
though she's different from Ophelia. She's cold, Skeet,
and never understood me. I see that now. If she had,
she'd never let her mother keep her away from me.
Nothin' can keep a girl away from you that loves you.
And I'll tell you something right now. Not long ago,
I was walkin' by her house on purpose and she came out
goin' somewhere. I tried to talk to her, and tell her
that we could meet sometimes, maybe down at Fillmore
Springs, or take a little walk at dusk or early evening;
and that I wouldn't bother her much, only we'd understand that by and by we'd get married and be together
forever, and I'd go away happy if I could have that hope.
Well, she kind of turned on me and said 'no,' and hurried
on. And, Skeet, when I saw that, when I saw that it
was her as well as her ma that wanted me away, and
meant to keep away from me — something kind of
froze through me — or burned maybe, and then froze —
my heart got like a big stone, and I could see it just as
if it had been scalt and then turned white and shiny and
kind of numb like my foot I cut in two. I began to laugh
and since then I have been changed; and I'll never be
the same again. My ma said it was foolish, that I was
just a little boy and I'd grow up and it would all be
forgotten. But I know better — I'm Hamlet — and I
don't forget, and I never will. Do you remember one
time when you and I was out to your grandpa's farm
and Willie Wallace was settin' out trees?"

I said " yes."

R

"Well," says Mitch, "Willie Wallace that time cut a gash in a tree with the pruner while handlin' it and settin' it out. And he says to us, 'That tree will never get over that. By and by it will be a big scar, growin' big as the tree grows big, and grown over, maybe, but still a scar; or worse, it may stay open more or less and rain and frost will get in, and insects, and after a while it will be a great rotten place, a hole for a snake or a rat, or maybe a bird.' Well, pa says that Linkern lost Anne Rutledge and that he thinks Linkern's beautiful talk and wonderful words came from losin' Anne Rutledge. I don't quite see how — but if it did, then if a bird gets into the hole in the tree, that's a sign that you

LA BELLE DAME SANS MERCI

say somethin' or write somethin' because you've been gashed, just as pa says that Shakespeare wrote his wonderfulest plays and sonnets because he'd lost a woman. And sometimes I think I'm goin' to write something. I keep hearin' music all the time, and I try to write words down, but they don't mean anything; they are silly; so I tear 'em up."

So Mitch went on and he worried me. And I says: "Mitch, I'm goin' to say somethin' to you! Do you like me as much as you used to?"

"Every bit," says he. "Why?"

"Because," says I, "you don't always act the same. And besides, you keep goin' with Charley King and George Heigold — and — and —"

"And what?" says Mitch.

"And — I was afraid you liked 'em better'n me."

"Why," says Mitch, "them two boys is just grave diggers compared to you — or Rosencrantz and Guildenstern — while you are Horatio all the time."

He explained to me what he meant by this, which was that in " Hamlet," Hamlet talked to grave diggers and to two men named Rosencrantz and Guildenstern, without givin' a snap for 'em compared to Horatio.

Then I said, "I'm goin' out to the farm to-morrow. School will begin in about three weeks. I'm goin' out on my pony, and you can ride behind. And you'd better come. We'll have a lot of fun, and my uncle is goin' to take me campin' to Blue Lake." So Mitch said he'd go; and after a bit he began to repeat something he'd committed to memory. He was settin' in the grass, lookin' up at me, and his voice was so wonderful and sweet, sayin' these words:

> O, what can ail thee, knight at arms,
> Alone and palely loitering?
> The sedge is withered from the lake,
> And no birds sing.
>
> O, what can ail thee, knight at arms,
> So haggard and so woe-begone?
> The squirrel's granary is full,
> And the harvest's done.
>
> "I met a lady in the meads
> Full beautiful, a faery's child.

> Her hair was long, her foot was light,
> And her eyes were wild.

> "I saw pale kings and warriors too,
> Pale princes, death pale were they all.
> They said ' La Belle Dame sans Merci
> Hath thee in thrall.' "

Mitch was goin' on with this when we heard some boys whistle. It was Charley King and George Heigold. They called Mitch to the fence and talked. Then Mitch called back and said, "I'm goin', Skeet — come for me — what time?"

"I'll be up about seven," I said.

And Mitch climbed over the fence, and went with these boys.

I went up to the fence and follered them with my eyes till they turned the corner by Harris' barn and was gone.

CHAPTER XXIX

T HE next morning I was on my pony and up to Mitch's house at seven, and whistled and whistled. By and by one of the girls came out and said Mitch had staid all night at Charley King's and wasn't home yet. So I went over there; but he and Charley was up and gone already. Mrs. King came to the door, came out and stood by the pony and petted him and said I had pretty eyes, same as before. Then she said Charley and Mitch had gone somewhere. She didn't know where. So I rode off and rode around a bit and then I started for the farm, thinkin' that Mitch had treated me mean — and why would he for Rosencrantz or Guildenstern? whichever Charley King was. I was sure Mitch would turn up and the next day grandpa was goin' to town early to be home by three o'clock, and he said he'd bring Mitch out if he could find him.

My uncle now was in a mood to go camping to Blue Lake. So we got the tent out and began to mend it where it needed it, and fix the ropes. We took the guns and cleaned 'em, and I helped my uncle load a lot of shells. We set aside some pie plates and cups and did a lot of tinkerin' around. Grandma didn't want us to go. She was afraid we'd get drowned or shoot ourselves, or that a storm would come up and we'd get struck by lightning.

In the afternoon old Washington Engle came and he and grandpa sat under the maple trees and talked old times, even about Indians, for they had been in the Black Hawk War together, and they had seen the country grow from buffalo grass to blue grass and clover. I sat there listenin'; and pretty soon a buggy pulled up and somebody called in a loud voice and laughed. It was John Armstrong and Aunt Caroline. They had drove over to visit; and John had brought his fiddle to play some of the old things for grandma — some of the things he had played years before when Aunt Mary was sick and grandma was takin' care of her. Grandpa liked gospel tunes, like "Swing Low, Sweet Chariot," but grandma liked "Rocky Road to Jordan" and "The Speckled Hen"; and John could play these and couldn't play religious tunes worth a cent. And John told stories as before; and he told about a man at Oakford who never had any money and always wanted drinks. So he took a jug and filled it half full of water and went to Porky Jim Thomas' saloon and asked for a half a gallon of alcohol, and Porky Jim poured it in. Then this man said to Porky Jim, "Charge it, please," and Porky Jim says: "Why, you ain't got a cent, and you never pay anybody." So he took up the jug and poured out what he had poured in and told the man to take the jug and go. And he did and had, of course, a half gallon all mixed. John laughed terribly at his own story — the women didn't laugh, nor grandpa. My uncle did, and I that's all.

Then Aunt Caroline helped grandma get supper and we had a lot of fun and they drove home.

The next day grandpa started early for Petersburg, so as to be back by three o'clock for something. And my uncle and me was getting ready because we was goin' to drive to Blue Lake that night, pitch the camp, and fish while it was quiet. So we had to grease the wagon and do a lot of things. And grandpa was to bring Mitch.

Three o'clock looked like it never would come. But at last about three I saw the white horses on the far hill, and then I saw them pulling hard and slow up the near hill and I could see grandpa now but couldn't see Mitch; and I watched and looked. Then I thought he was hid under the seat; or had dropped off to walk and come in later and fool me.

Grandpa drove in the lot. His face was set. He looked serious. He didn't look at me. He held the lines and looked straight ahead. I climbed on the carriage and says, "Where's Mitch?" Just then my uncle came up to unhitch the horses. My grandpa threw him the lines and grandpa got out of the carriage. Then he said, speaking really to my uncle and not to me:

"Mitchie Miller was killed this afternoon on the railroad."

"Grandpa!" I cried. "Grandpa!"

My grandfather's eyes were purple — they had grown deep and almost terrible to see. And he said: "Yes, son," and hurried toward the house.

I went to the barn. I saddled and bridled my pony. I leaped into the saddle and struck my heels into the pony's flanks, and away I went in a run all the way to Petersburg — six miles and not a pause or a let up.

When I got there in a little more than half an hour, I found that they had Mitch up at the house of Widow Morris. So I went there. He was still alive — and they

let me in. It was terrible. Such a smell of ether —
medicines. Such whisperings — such fullness in the
room. The doctor said we'd have to clear out, some of
us. And some left. I staid long enough to see Mitch.
His eyes were closed. His face was yellow — I could see
blood. I turned sick and went out of the room. Just
as I got to the door I heard Mitch say, "Has pa come?"
They said, "He's comin', Mitchie, be patient, he's
comin'." Then I stood by the door.

And pretty soon Mrs. Miller came and the girls and
my mother and Myrtle and most every one. It seemed
Mr. Miller was away selling atlases, but would be home
soon, maybe, or maybe not till late, and maybe not till
to-morrow. All the girls cried like their hearts would
break; and Mrs. Miller knelt down by the bed, and
Mitch says to her, "Where's pa?" And she says, "He's
comin', Mitchie." And then she choked and had to walk
away. They cleared the room now pretty much, and of
course Mrs. Miller allowed me to be in the room if I
wanted to, and could stand it. But I stood by the door,
or just inside a little, for Mitch was talkin'. Finally
they let me go to the bed-side, and Mitch saw me and
says, "Skeet," and then turned his head kind of over
as if he wanted to say something he couldn't bear
to say.

Then Mitch began to talk more. "Don't row so fast,"
he'd say — "The river's gettin' swifter. Take the horses
from that engine. I'm goin' to see Tom Sawyer — I can
fly to him — fly — fly — fly — Zueline — it's you, is
it?"

Then he kind of woke up and says: "Is Zueline
here?" And they said, "No, but she was comin';" but
she wasn't; she was out of town, and probably wouldn't

have come anyway. And then he said — "Get my pa —
he must forgive me before I die."

By this time I knew how Mitch was hurt. He'd been
with Charley King and George Heigold, and they had
been flippin' on the train. And Mitch was ridin' on the

MITCH SAW ME AND SAYS, "SKEET"

side of a car with his foot hangin' down that he had
cut in two, draggin' against the wheel, which he didn't
notice because his foot was numb from being cut in
two when he was four or five years old. So the train
gave a lurch and dragged him under; and the wheels
cut him at the hip. It couldn't be amputated by the
doctor, and they couldn't stop the bleedin'.

Then Mitch began to repeat all kinds of poetry from
" Hamlet " and things I didn't know ; and he repeated
what he had recited to me that day :

> "I saw pale kings and warriors too,
> Pale princes, death pale were they all.
> They said 'La Belle Dame sans Merci
> Hath thee in thrall.'"

And he talked about flyin', about treasure, about St.
Louis, about Doc Lyon, and Joe Rainey and the pistol ;
and once he talked as if he thought he was testifyin' in
court ; and he said — "Now we're on the Mississippi —
how fast the boat goes — don't row so fast." But always
he'd come to and say, " Where's my pa ? "

And after a bit there was a stir — Mr. Miller came —
pushed his way through. He was pale as ashes, all
trembling, out of breath, for he'd run up the hill. And
he came to the bedside, but Mitch was dreaming again,
drifting and dreaming, and talking about boats, about
money, about Hamlet, about treasure, about pale
kings and warriors and death-pale princes. But pretty
soon he says, "Where's my pa ? Is he never
comin' ? "

"I'm here," said Mr. Miller.

Mitch opened his eyes and looked at his father for
about a minute and saw his pa had come. He was pretty
weak now and it was hard for him to speak. But finally
he said, "Take my hand — pa." And Mr. Miller took
it. And then nothin' was said for a while. And then
Mitch spoke again — "Forgive me, pa." And Mr.
Miller, who was tryin' to keep from cryin' so as not to
worry Mitch, says, "Oh yes, Mitchie." And then Mitch
says : "Say a little prayer, pa." And Mr. Miller knelt

by the bed to say a prayer, and Mitch says — "Not out loud — just to yourself."

So Mr. Miller did, and then Mitch wandered again and he says, "Don't row so fast." Then there was a terrible stillness. Mitch had died with them words.

And my friend — my chum, was gone for good.

CHAPTER XXX

AND then there was the funeral. It was held at Mr. Miller's house and everybody was there; my grandpa, my grandma, my uncle, John Armstrong and Aunt Caroline, Willie Wallace, Colonel Lambkin, Nigger Dick, Dinah, my ma and Myrtle, all the Sunday School children, and George Montgomery. Only Charley King and George Heigold wasn't there. They were afraid, bein' partly responsible for Mitch's death. And when everybody was seated and ready, Zueline and her ma came. They was all dressed up, and everybody looked at 'em. Mr. Miller, of course, couldn't preach the sermon for his own boy; so they sent for a wonderful preacher over at Jacksonville and he talked for about an hour about pearly gates and the golden streets of Paradise; and there was Mitch lyin' there, pale, his eyes sealed, just asleep, but in such a deep, breathless sleep. And they had the church choir there which sang. And one of the songs they sang was:

I will sing you a song of that beautiful land,
Of the far away home of the soul,
Where no storms ever beat on that glittering strand,
While the years of eternity roll.

And the minister went on to say how good God was, how no sparrow falls except He knows it, how all our hairs was numbered and how God loves us, and would comfort the father and mother and brothers and sisters, and little friends; and how if it hadn't been for the best, Mitch wouldn't have died; and that God knew best and we didn't; and if we could look ahead and see the dreadful things that would happen, we'd know that God was good and wise to take Mitch away before they happened — while he was yet a boy, and had had no trouble and all the world was still beautiful to him. And he talked about sin and what suffering does for people, how it makes 'em humble before God, and respectful and at last saves 'em if they will heed the lessons and turn to God. Everybody cried when the last song was sung, especially the children, who sobbed out loud, and Mr. Miller and Mrs. Miller and the Miller children — and I looked over at Zueline and her ma. Her ma was just lookin' down. I thought I saw a tear in Zueline's eyes, but I'm not sure. So we went out to the cemetery and they buried Mitch not far from Little Billie. So it was all over. We began to separate and get into carriages or walk. And pretty soon I was home. There was nothing there. My ma went in and began to do something. Myrtle went out to the swing. I went in the house but couldn't stand it; and then came out and hung on the gate.

After a bit Charley King came along and asked me about everything. Pa said Mitch had been running with Charley King and George Heigold, and they got him into things too much for his age, flippin' cars and such things, and that's how Mitch lost his life. You see I'd been scared about this; I didn't want Mitch to go with 'em; I didn't know why; but now it was clear.

And with everything else, it was Sunday, for Mitch
had died Friday, four or five hours after he was run
over. And it was only a week now till school would
take up.

The next day I went down to the office with pa. I
wanted to be close to him; he was a man; he was
strong, and I was lonesome and grievin', and at night
always dreamin' of Mitch. And after a while Mr. Miller
came in, and Mrs. Miller too. They looked terrible sad
and pale. Here was Mr. Miller out of a church and not
makin' much, and here they had lost their only boy.

So pa went over to his safe and got the $1000; he
had it in two envelopes, one marked with my name and
one with Mitch's; and he came back, holdin' 'em in
his hand and he said: "You know that these boys
found that money that belonged to old Nancy Allen.
Well, a fellow named Joe Allen turned up here from
Pike County — a third cousin of hers — and her only
livin' relative, and I had this money for him. But when
I told him that these boys had found it while lookin'
for treasure, and what kind of boys they were, the old
fellow remembered his own boyhood, his poverty, and
all that and he wanted to do something for these boys.
So he made me take this thousand dollars to divide
between 'em." Mrs. Miller began to sob. And Mr.
Miller's voice was broken, but he said, "Hard, I never
heard anything like this — never in my life." "Well,
here's the money," says pa; "and I made Skeet promise
not to tell anybody about it until we got ready to."
He stopped; and I, not thinkin', said: "It was to be a
secret till Christmas."

Then Mrs. Miller broke down completely, and for
several minutes nothin' was said. My pa was cryin',

so was I. So was Mr. Miller, and just then the train came in, the same that had killed Mitch, and it seemed like none of us could stand it.

After a bit pa says: "Of course, half of this money goes to you and Mrs. Miller under the law, and the other half belongs to Skeet — but I'm not going to let him take it. He doesn't need it. I can always take care of him, and I'll inherit quite a lot, and he'll have that. And as far as that goes, it wasn't his idea to hunt for treasure — he was just a helper and followed up Mitchie's idea. So now here it is, and it goes with my blessing and with Skeet's."

And I said, "Indeed it does." And pa handed the envelopes to Mr. Miller, and he took 'em and fingered 'em in a nervous way and he says: "What shall we do, ma? — we need the money, but somehow I don't like it, and I won't take Skeet's share, would you?"

And she says, "No — never — I'd never take Skeet's share; that is Mitchie's share and his too." "Here," he says, "here's the envelope marked with Mitchie's name, you take this, Skeet, because you and Mitchie worked together, and if you want to give me the envelope marked with your name, I guess I'll take it— I seem to have to."

So that's the way it was done. And he said to pa: "Hard, there never was a better man than you, or a better name or family than yours, or a better boy than Skeet." Then the tears came in his eyes, and he and Mrs. Miller left. And afterwards I said to pa, "I don't want this money. If I could have had it with Mitch, if we could have spent it together for velocipedes — and dogs, and sets of tools, for scroll saws, watches and whatever we wanted, and soda water, when we wanted it, and bananas, which we never had much because they cost ten cents apiece — for anything, that would have been different. But now it's just so much rags or paper, and I haven't got any use for it whatever. I am Huck Finn at last — the money means nothing to me. It meant nothing to Huck, because when he got it, he had to put on shoes and dress up. And now I've got it, I've lost the only thing that made it worth while. I've lost Mitch who made it interestin' to get, and would have made it interestin' to spend."

Then I told pa I wanted to give it to the Miller girls, barrin' just a few dollars to buy a present for ma and grandma and Myrtle, maybe — and I wanted them to take enough to put up a stone at Mitch's grave with some words on it, suitable to him.

So pa said he thought that was all right. And I took out $20 and we put the rest in the bank in the names of the Miller girls — and that ended the treasure.

So next Monday school commenced, and I sat in my seat lookin' out of the window. Zueline had been taken to a girls' school in Springfield so as to get her out of the common schools; and her mother had gone with her to stay all winter. And every day the train came through that Mitch was killed on. The days went by; the fall went by; the winter came. The snow began to fall on Mitch's grave and Little Billie's; and still we went on. Delia got the meals as before; the washwoman came and did the washing on Monday; pa was buying wood for the stoves; we had to be fitted out for winter. Grandma and grandpa came in to see us, cheerful and kind as they always were. Once he carried a half a pig up the hill and brought it to us; and they were always giving us things; and grandma was always knitting

me mittens and socks. They had lost a lot of children, two little girls the same summer, a daughter who was grown, a grown son who was drowned. They seemed to take Mitchie's death and Little Billie's death as natural and to be stood. And they said it wouldn't be long before we'd all be together, never to be separated; and then we'd all be really happy.

And finally the December court came around and they tried Temple Scott. Harold Carman testified to what he had said to the woman on the boat. And Major Abbott was kerflummoxed and lost the case. Temple Scott got fourteen years in prison — and that ended that. He went there and staid.

And then Christmas came and in the evening I went up to the Millers'. The girls were playing about the same as before. Mr. Miller was reading Shakespeare to Mrs. Miller and he looked up finally and said, "Ma, I've just thought of an epitaph for Mitchie's stone — here it is in 'Hamlet': 'The rest is silence.'" And Mrs. Miller said " yes " and put her knitting down to count stitches. The girls rushed into the room laughing and chasing each other. And then I went home.

I had presents, but what was presents? My chum was gone. I thought of the last Christmas when we was all together — Mitch was here then and Little Billie. I couldn't enjoy anything. I crept up to bed and fell asleep and dreamed of Mitch.

You will be surprised to know how I came to write this story. But before I tell you that I want to say that if Mitch had written it, it would have been much better. I sit here, dipping my nose in the Gascon wine, so to speak, as Thackeray wrote of himself; and I

s

know now that Mitch was a poet. He would have made poems out of his life and mine, beautiful songs of this country, of Illinois, of the people we knew, of the honest, kindly men and women we knew; the sweet-faced old women who were born in Kentucky or Tennessee, or came here to Illinois early in their youth; the strong, courtly, old-fashioned men, carrying with them the early traditions of the republic, in their way Lincolns — honest, truth telling, industrious, courageous Americans — plain and unlettered, many of them, but full of the sterling virtues. Yes, he would have written poems out of these people; and he would have done something more — he would have given us symbols, songs of eternal truth, of unutterable magic and profound meaning like "La Belle Dame sans Merci." I am sure he would have done something of this kind — though it is idle to say he would have written anything as immortal as that. You must only indulge me in my partiality for Mitch, and my belief in his genius, and hope with me that he might have done these great things.

And yet! And now why did I write this story? As I was sitting with my nose in the Gascon wine, which is a strange figure, since there is no Gascon wine here, and no wine of any sort, since a strange sort of despot has got control of the country, for the time being only, I hope — as I said, as I was sitting with my nose in the Gascon wine, I was also reading, and I was alone. I have had chums, I have had companions, but none like Mitch, never in all my life. And being alone, I was reading — what do you suppose? I had been out for the evening, I had found a book lying on the table of my host, I had looked in the book and begun to read. My host saw I was intrigued and said, "Take it along."

I did, and was reading before going to bed. The book was the letters of John Keats to Fannie Brawne.— Well, don't you suppose these letters made me think of Mitch who had repeated "La Belle Dame sans Merci" to me and was uttering some of its marvelous lines with his dying breath? But this was not all. Let me quote one of Keats' letters to Fanny Brawne:

"When you were in the habit of flirting with Brown, you would have left off, could your own heart have felt one half of one pang mine did. Brown is a good sort of man — he did not know he was doing me to death by inches. I feel the effect of every one of those hours in my side now; and for that cause, though he has done me many services, though I know his love and friendship for me, though at this moment I should be without pence were it not for his assistance, I will never see or speak to him, until we are both old men, if we are to be. I will resent my heart having been made a football. You will call this madness. I have heard you say that it was not unpleasant to wait a few years — you have amusements — your mind is away, — you have not brooded over one idea as I have, and how should you? You are to me an object intensely desirable — the air I breathe in a room empty of you is unhealthy. I am not the same to you — no — you can wait — you have a thousand activities — you can be happy without me. Any party, any thing to fill up the day has been enough. How have you passed this month? Who have you smiled with? All this may seem savage in me. You do not feel as I do — you do not know what it is to love — one day you may — your time is not come. Ask yourself how many unhappy hours Keats has caused you in loneliness. For myself I have been a martyr the whole time, and for this reason I speak; the confession is forced from me by the torture. I appeal to you by the blood of Christ you believe in. Do not write to me if you have done anything this month which it would have harried me to have seen. You may have altered — if you have not — if you still behave in dancing rooms and other societies as I have seen you — I do not want to live — if you have done so, I wish this coming night may be my last. I cannot live without you and not only you but chaste you; virtuous you. The sun rises and sets, the day passes, and you follow the bent of your inclinations to a certain extent — you have no conception of the quantity of miserable feeling that passes through me in a day — Be serious Love is not a plaything — and again do not write unless you can do it with a crystal conscience. I would sooner die for want of you than —

"Yours forever,

"J. KEATS."

Then I turned back a few pages in my disconnected way of reading this book, and I found these words: Fannie Brawne to whom this agonized letter of Keats' was written wrote to a Mr. Dilke ten years after Keats' death in regard to a memoir proposed to the dead, and in the following unconcerned and ignorant way:

"The kindest act would be to let him rest forever in the obscurity to which circumstances have condemned him."

No remembrance here for Keats' adoration; no thrill that a human heart, even if it had been the heart of an ordinary man, had poured out its last devotion to hers; no pity for his obscurity, if it was such, his untimely and tragic death; no recognition of his passion for beauty, including his misguided passion for the beauty which was not in her; no perception of the goodness in the man, the bravery of his heart; the white fire of his spirit; no understanding of his greatness, even after Byron had written that "Hyperion" was as sublime as Æschylus, and Shelley had poured out in "Adonais" the grief and the passion of a flaming indignation and scorn in one of the greatest of elegies; no memory con-

templating the agony of a dying youth stricken with
consumption, and torn with the tragic spectacle of
defeated ambition. "Let him rest forever in the
obscurity to which circumstances have condemned
him." — These were her words in the face of all these
things.

And so, reading these words of Fanny Brawne, my
mind turned back to Mitch, and his life rose before me
and took shape in my mind, and I wrote; just because
he had had this boyhood love for Zueline and went
through that summer of torture for losing her. And I
could see that he might have suffered these pangs again;
that over and over again, perhaps, he might have poured
out his passion in the endless search for beauty and faith,
and in the search for realization and glimpses of eternal
things through them, and that he would have never
found them, through woman; and so thinking I could
look back upon his death at twelve years of age with
complacency, and almost with gladness.

But also if he had lived through as many years as I
have lived, he would have passed through the chaos,
the dust, the hate, the untruth that followed the Civil
War. He would have seen an army organization exer-
cising a control in the affairs of the republic beyond
its right, and ideas that were dead and were never right-
fully alive, keeping the people of his country from pulling
themselves out of poverties and injustices, and from
planting themselves upon the new soil of each succeeding
year and its needs. He would have seen wealth amass
through legalized privilege into the hands of treasure
hunters; and he would have seen these treasure hunters
make and interpret the laws their own way, and in
behalf of the treasure they had and were seeking. He

would have seen his country go forth to free an island people, and then turn and subjugate another island people as a part of the same war, and then depart from the old ways into paths of world adventure and plunder. And he would have seen his country spend ten times what it spent in the Civil War and lose in battles or disease half as many young men as it lost in the Civil War in the crusade of making the world safe for democracy; and he would have seen democracy throttled and almost destroyed at home, and democracy abroad helped no whit by this terrible war. He would have seen that all these things happen for treasure — for gold which cares nothing for laws, nothing for liberties, nothing for beauty, nothing for human life, but always seeks its own everywhere and always, which is its own increase and its own conservation. He would have seen men jailed for nothing and sacred rights swept away by the sneers of judges, and written safeguards of the people's liberties by those very judges sworn to support, overthrown by them, at the bidding of treasure hunters who stand back of hired orators, hired newspapers, hired clergymen, hired lawyers, and hired officials. He would have seen congresses uttering and acting upon lies, and his country bound together with a network of elaborate falsehood.

The America his father hoped for and the America he would have hoped for sits for the time being, anyway, in dullness and in dust. And so I am not sorry that for these nearly thirty years, Mitchie Miller has been dust, a part of the hill overlooking the Sangamon River, not far from the deserted village of Old Salem— his dust at one with the hill and sharing its own eternity!

Printed in the United States of America.